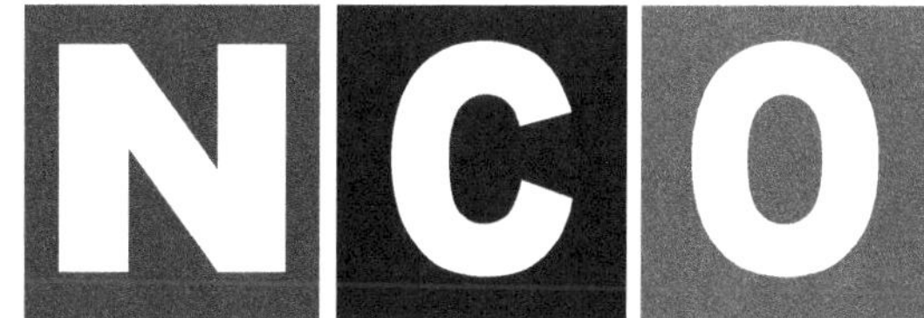

OLYMPIAD WORKBOOK

NATIONAL CYBER OLYMPIAD

- **01** Learning Objectives
- **02** Multiple Choice Questions
- **03** HOTS (Achievers Section)
- **04** Model Test Paper
- **05** Answer Keys and Solutions
- **06** OMR Answer Sheet

V&S PUBLISHERS

Published by:

V&S PUBLISHERS

F-2/16, Ansari road, Daryaganj, New Delhi-110002
☎ 23240026, 23240027 • *Fax:* 011-23240028
✉ info@vspublishers.com • ⊕ www.vspublishers.com

Online Brandstore: amazon.in/vspublishers

Regional Office : Hyderabad
5-1-707/1, Brij Bhawan (Beside Central Bank of India Lane)
Bank Street, Koti, Hyderabad - 500 095
☎ 040-24737290
✉ vspublishershyd@gmail.com

Follow us on:   

BUY OUR BOOKS FROM: AMAZON FLIPKART

DISCLAIMER

While every attempt has been made to provide accurate and timely information in this book, neither the author nor the publisher assumes any responsibility for errors, unintended omissions or commissions detected therein. The author and publisher makes no representation or warranty with respect to the comprehensiveness or completeness of the contents provided.

All matters included have been simplified under professional guidance for general information only, without any warranty for applicability on an individual. Any mention of an organization or a website in the book, by way of citation or as a source of additional information, doesn't imply the endorsement of the content either by the author or the publisher. It is possible that websites cited may have changed or removed between the time of editing and publishing the book.

Results from using the expert opinion in this book will be totally dependent on individual circumstances and factors beyond the control of the author and the publisher.

It makes sense to elicit advice from well informed sources before implementing the ideas given in the book. The reader assumes full responsibility for the consequences arising out from reading this book.

For proper guidance, it is advisable to read the book under the watchful eyes of parents/guardian. The buyer of this book assumes all responsibility for the use of given materials and information.

The copyright of the entire content of this book rests with the author/publisher. Any infringement/transmission of the cover design, text or illustrations, in any form, by any means, by any entity will invite legal action and be responsible for consequences thereon.

PUBLISHER'S NOTE

V&S Publishers has carved a significant niche in the publishing industry over the last decade, having successfully published more than 1000 titles across 9 languages spanning over 50 subject categories. Being known for the quality of content, we have built a reputation of excellence and reliability. We have consistently delivered **"Value & Substance"** to our readers, through a wide range of titles across a variety of genres covering school books, fiction and non-fiction that caters to different people from every section of the society.

The **Olympiad Guidebooks for classes 1-10** across all subjects, launched almost a decade ago, under the **GEN X Imprint**, became a go-to-source for the school students in no time, owing to their invaluable and substantive content written in a guidebook pattern,.

Having successfully sold a million copies of the same and in response to demand by both students as well as shopkeepers nationwide; we now present before you our newly launched **Olympiad Workbook Series**, designed for **classes 1-10 across 4 subjects**.

The workbooks are meticulously curated by a team of experienced educators, researchers and subject matter experts, edited by professionals and peer reviewed by teachers. The team has poured its efforts and expertise into creating a crisp and concise workbook which will help and guide the students to the path of success in Olympiad exams. The **MCQs** identified will not only help in scoring top marks in Olympiads but also inculcate a sense of deeper understanding of the subject, by way of solving **HOTS** and referring to complete solutions at the end of the book.

Here we present our new release– **OLYMPIAD WORKBOOK (NCO) CLASS–10** having following features:

- ☞ Based on the latest syllabi
- ☞ MCQs with comprehensive coverage of topics
- ☞ HOTS Questions liberally included
- ☞ A dedicated chapter on logical reasoning
- ☞ Model test paper for thorough practice
- ☞ Sample OMR sheet for real time simulation

We have made sure through our best efforts, that this workbook strictly follows the latest syllabi and patterns of the Olympiad Examination.

As **V&S Publishers** continuously strive to enhance the readability and maintain the credibility of our academic publications, we seek the support of our valuable readers in influencing and enriching the lives of future generations of students.

P.S. While every care has been taken to ensure the correctness of the content, if you come across any error, howsoever minor, do not hesitate to discuss with teachers while pointing that out to us in no uncertain terms.

We wish you all the best for your exams!

DISTINCTIVE FEATURES

01 — Learning Objectives

They list the whole chapter as subtopics, helping the teachers to guide children in a step-by-step manner.

02 — Multiple Choice Questions

MCQs act as an excellent learning aid, helping you to understand and work on your mistakes.

03 — HOTS (Achievers Section)

The High Order Thinking Questions aim to help the student to solve Application-based questions and gain practical understanding of the subject.

04 — Model Test Paper

Model test paper are provided at the end of each book, which help the student to test the knowledge which they have gained after thorough reading of all chapters.

05 — Answer Key

Detailed Answer Key along with explanations aid the pupil to indentify, understand the mistakes they make during the course of Olympiad preparation.

CONTENTS

FUNDAMENTALS OF COMPUTER

LEARNING OBJECTIVES

- ➤ Characteristics of Computers
- ➤ Limitations of Computer
- ➤ Parts of Computer
- ➤ Classification of Computer
- ➤ Types of Software
- ➤ Types of Language

MULTIPLE CHOICE QUESTIONS

1. In order to play and hear sound on a computer, one needs:
   (A) A sound card and speakers
   (B) A microphone
   (C) All of them required
   (D) None of them required

2. Cursor is a ______.
   (A) Pixel
   (B) Thin blinking line
   (C) Pointing device
   (D) None of these

3. Which device is required for the Internet connection?
   (A) Joystick   (B) Modem
   (C) CD Drive   (D) NIC Card

4. The digital signals can be represented by
   (A) Binary Codes   (B) 0 and 1
   (C) High and Low   (D) All of these

5. Modulator-demodulator is a device that converts
   (A) Digital signal into analog signal
   (B) Analog signal into digital signal
   (C) Both (A) and (B)
   (D) None of these

6. Actual execution of instructions in a computer takes place in
   (A) ALU
   (B) Control Unit
   (C) Storage unit
   (D) None of these

7. The communication line between the CPU, memory and peripherals is called a
   (A) Bus
   (B) Line
   (C) Media
   (D) None of these

8. A computer cannot "boot" if it does not have the
   (A) Compiler
   (B) Loader
   (C) Operating system
   (D) Assembler

9. A bootstrap is:
   (A) a memory device
   (B) a device to support the computer
   (C) a small initialisation program to start up a computer
   (D) an error correction technique

10. Which of the following is not a hardware:?
    (A) Magnetic tape   (B) Printer
    (C) VDU terminal   (D) Assembler

11. The operating system is also called the _______between the user and the computer.
    (A) Interface
    (B) Interrelate
    (C) Interference
    (D) Intermediate

12. When installing a peripheral, you also usually need to install a _______.
    (A) port
    (B) server
    (C) password
    (D) driver

13. Computers use which of the following number systems to store information?
    (A) base 2
    (B) base 4
    (C) base 8
    (D) base 10

14. Internet safety relates to _______.
    (A) only those who buy products online
    (B) only those who do their banking online
    (C) only those who sign up for chat rooms
    (D) everyone who uses a computer that can connect to the Internet

15. A KB represents _______ bytes.
    (A) 8
    (B) 1,000
    (C) 1,000,000
    (D) 1,000,000,000

16. Which feature allows the user to view information about his computer hardware?
    (A) Start
    (B) My Computer
    (C) Control Panel
    (D) All Programs

17. The size of the monitor is determined by measuring the screen _______.
    (A) Vertically, from top to bottom
    (B) Horizontally, from left to right
    (C) Diagonally, from the top left corner to the bottom right corner
    (D) None of these

18. SMPS stands for
    (A) Switched Mode Power Supply
    (B) Simple Mode Power Supply
    (C) Simple Made Power Supply
    (D) None of these

19. Which of the following is NOT a type of motherboard expansion slot?
    (A) ISA
    (B) PCI
    (C) AGP
    (D) ATX

20. Which of the following retains the information it's storing when the power to the system is turned OFF?
    (A) CPU
    (B) ROM
    (C) DRAM
    (D) DIMM

21. What type of connector is used to plug a telephone line into a modem?
    (A) COM1
    (B) RJ-11
    (C) RJ-45
    (D) RJ-10

22. BIOS stands for
    (A) bootstrap initial operating system
    (B) basic input output startup
    (C) boot initial operating startup
    (D) basic input output system

23. What is the data transfer rate for USB 2.0?
    (A) 480Mbs   (B) 512Mbs
    (C) 520Mbs   (D) none of these

24. Portable pen drive connects to the _____ port of computer
    (A) USB 2.0
    (B) USB
    (C) USB 5.0
    (D) None of these

25. With reference to a CPU, What does MIPS mean?
    (A) Million Instructions Per Second
    (B) Million Per Second Instruction
    (C) Micro Instructions Per Second
    (D) Macro Instructions Per Second

26. UPS stands for:
    (A) Universal Power Supply
    (B) Uninterruptible Power Supply
    (C) Unique Power Supply
    (D) Unconditional Power Supply

27. From what location are the 1st computer instructions available on boot up?
    (A) ROM BIOS
    (B) CPU
    (C) boot.ini
    (D) CONFIG.SYS

28. Missing slot covers on a computer can cause
    (A) Overheat
    (B) Power surges
    (C) EMI
    (D) incomplete path for ESD

29. IDE cables have how many pins?
    (A) 25
    (B) 50
    (C) 100
    (D) 40

30. How many pins are there on a VGA?
    (A) 15
    (B) 9
    (C) 25
    (D) 32

HOTS (ACHIEVERS SECTION)

31. When the computer you are using does not print, what is the likely reason?
    (A) The printer is not plugged in to either the power or to your computer.
    (B) You have not selected the correct printer from the list.
    (C) There is a printer jam or the printer needs some other attention.
    (D) All of these

32. A computer sometimes 'freezes' so that the programs that are running are no longer usable. What must a user do when her computer 'freezes'?
    (A) Keep pressing the <enter> key until the computer restarts
    (B) Press 'CRTL' + 'ALT' + 'Delete' to view the task manager.
    (C) Press 'Delete' to restart your computer
    (D) None of these

33. Which device you should use to prevent the effect of power fluctuation in the power supply on your computer and works for a specific period of time even there is no power?
    (A) SMPS
    (B) UPS
    (C) Hard disk
    (D) ROM

34. IBM launched its first personal computer called IBM-PC in 1981. It had chips from Intel, disk drives from Tandon, operating system from Microsoft, the printer from Epson and the application software from everywhere. Can you name the country which contributed the video display?
    (A) India
    (B) China
    (C) Germany
    (D) Taiwan

35. What is an interpreter?
    (A) An interpreter does the conversion line by line as the program is run.
    (B) An interpreter is the representation of the system being designed.
    (C) An interpreter is a general purpose language providing very efficient execution.
    (D) None of these

36. The size of the dots in inkjet printer usually lies between
    (A) 50 to 60 microns in diameter
    (B) 20 to 30 microns in diameter
    (C) 30 to 40 microns in diameter
    (D) 10 to 20 microns in diameter

37. The following are the input devices.
    (A) Keyboard, Mouse, Scanner, Flatbed plotter
    (B) Scanner, Drum plotter, Mouse, Joystick
    (C) Keyboard, Mouse, Scanner, Flatbed scanner
    (D) None of these

38. Plotters can be generally divided into _______ categories namely _______.
    (A) Two, Pen, Plotters and Electrostatic
    (B) Two, Drum, Plotters and Flatbed
    (C) Four, Pen, Electrostatic, Drum and Flatbed
    (D) Three, Pen, Electrostatic and Flatbed

39. Which of the following is the first neural network computer?
    (A) AN   (B) AM
    (C) RFD   (D) SNARC

40. OMR, OCR, and MICR are all types of:
    (A) Radio frequency card readers (RFID.
    (B) Magnetic card readers.
    (C) Bar code readers.
    (D) Character and mark recognition devices.

---Darken Your Choice with HB Pencil---

1.	Ⓐ Ⓑ Ⓒ Ⓓ	9.	Ⓐ Ⓑ Ⓒ Ⓓ	17.	Ⓐ Ⓑ Ⓒ Ⓓ	25	Ⓐ Ⓑ Ⓒ Ⓓ	33.	Ⓐ Ⓑ Ⓒ Ⓓ
2.	Ⓐ Ⓑ Ⓒ Ⓓ	10.	Ⓐ Ⓑ Ⓒ Ⓓ	18.	Ⓐ Ⓑ Ⓒ Ⓓ	26.	Ⓐ Ⓑ Ⓒ Ⓓ	34.	Ⓐ Ⓑ Ⓒ Ⓓ
3.	Ⓐ Ⓑ Ⓒ Ⓓ	11.	Ⓐ Ⓑ Ⓒ Ⓓ	19.	Ⓐ Ⓑ Ⓒ Ⓓ	27.	Ⓐ Ⓑ Ⓒ Ⓓ	35.	Ⓐ Ⓑ Ⓒ Ⓓ
4.	Ⓐ Ⓑ Ⓒ Ⓓ	12.	Ⓐ Ⓑ Ⓒ Ⓓ	20.	Ⓐ Ⓑ Ⓒ Ⓓ	28.	Ⓐ Ⓑ Ⓒ Ⓓ	36.	Ⓐ Ⓑ Ⓒ Ⓓ
5.	Ⓐ Ⓑ Ⓒ Ⓓ	13.	Ⓐ Ⓑ Ⓒ Ⓓ	21.	Ⓐ Ⓑ Ⓒ Ⓓ	29.	Ⓐ Ⓑ Ⓒ Ⓓ	37.	Ⓐ Ⓑ Ⓒ Ⓓ
6.	Ⓐ Ⓑ Ⓒ Ⓓ	14.	Ⓐ Ⓑ Ⓒ Ⓓ	22.	Ⓐ Ⓑ Ⓒ Ⓓ	30.	Ⓐ Ⓑ Ⓒ Ⓓ	38.	Ⓐ Ⓑ Ⓒ Ⓓ
7.	Ⓐ Ⓑ Ⓒ Ⓓ	15.	Ⓐ Ⓑ Ⓒ Ⓓ	23.	Ⓐ Ⓑ Ⓒ Ⓓ	31.	Ⓐ Ⓑ Ⓒ Ⓓ	39.	Ⓐ Ⓑ Ⓒ Ⓓ
8.	Ⓐ Ⓑ Ⓒ Ⓓ	16.	Ⓐ Ⓑ Ⓒ Ⓓ	24.	Ⓐ Ⓑ Ⓒ Ⓓ	32.	Ⓐ Ⓑ Ⓒ Ⓓ	40.	Ⓐ Ⓑ Ⓒ Ⓓ

OPERATING SYSTEMS

LEARNING OBJECTIVES

➤ Basics of operating system
➤ Different types of operating system

MULTIPLE CHOICE QUESTIONS

1. What is an operating system?
   (A) interface between the hardware and application programs
   (B) collection of programs that manages hardware resources
   (C) system service provider to the application programs
   (D) all of the mentioned

2. In Operating Systems, which of the following is/are CPU scheduling algorithms?
   (A) Priority
   (B) Round Robin
   (C) Shortest Job First
   (D) All of the mentioned

3. To access the services of the operating system, the interface is provided by the __________
   (A) Library
   (B) System calls
   (C) Assembly instructions
   (D) API

4. CPU scheduling is the basis of __________.
   (A) multiprogramming operating systems
   (B) larger memory sized systems
   (C) multiprocessor systems
   (D) none of the mentioned

5. Which one of the following is not true?
   (A) kernel remains in the memory during the entire computer session
   (B) kernel is made of various modules which can not be loaded in running operating system
   (C) kernel is the first part of the operating system to load into memory during booting
   (D) kernel is the program that constitutes the central core of the operating system

6. Which one of the following errors will be handle by the operating system?
   (A) lack of paper in printer
   (B) connection failure in the network
   (C) power failure
   (D) all of the mentioned

7. Where is the operating system placed in the memory?
   (A) either low or high memory (depending on the location of interrupt vector)
   (B) in the low memory
   (C) in the high memory
   (D) none of the mentioned

8. If a process fails, most operating system write the error information to a _______
   (A) new file
   (B) another running process
   (C) log file
   (D) none of the mentioned

9. In operating system, each process has its own __________
   (A) open files
   (B) pending alarms, signals, and signal handlers
   (C) address space and global variables
   (D) all of the mentioned

10. In a timeshare operating system, when the time slot assigned to a process is completed, the process switches from the current state to?
    (A) Suspended state
    (B) Terminated state
    (C) Ready state
    (D) Blocked state

11. When a process is in a "Blocked" state waiting for some I/O service. When the service is completed, it goes to the __________
    (A) Terminated state
    (B) Suspended state
    (C) Running state
    (D) Ready state

12. The portion of the process scheduler in an operating system that dispatches processes is concerned with __________
    (A) assigning ready processes to waiting queue
    (B) assigning running processes to blocked queue
    (C) assigning ready processes to CPU
    (D) all of the mentioned

13. The FCFS algorithm is particularly troublesome for __________
    (A) operating systems
    (B) multiprocessor systems
    (C) time sharing systems
    (D) multiprogramming systems

14. A deadlock avoidance algorithm dynamically examines the __________ to ensure that a circular wait condition can never exist.
    (A) operating system
    (B) resources
    (C) system storage state
    (D) resource allocation state

15. Swapping __________ be done when a process has pending I/O, or has to execute I/O operations only into operating system buffers.
    (A) must never   (B) maybe
    (C) can   (D) must

16. The main memory accommodates __________.
    (A) cpu
    (B) user processes
    (C) operating system
    (D) all of the mentioned

17. The operating system is responsible for?
    (A) bad-block recovery
    (B) booting from disk
    (C) disk initialization
    (D) all of the mentioned

18. The operating system and the other processes are protected from being modified by an already running process because __________
    (A) every address generated by the CPU is being checked against the relocation and limit registers
    (B) they have a protection algorithm
    (C) they are in different memory spaces
    (D) they are in different logical addresses

19. The operating system maintains a _______ table that keeps track of how many frames have been allocated, how many are there, and how many are available.
    (A) memory   (B) mapping
    (C) page   (D) frame

20. In real time operating system __________.
    (A) process scheduling can be done only once
    (B) all processes have the same priority
    (C) kernel is not required
    (D) a task must be serviced by its deadline period

21. For real time operating systems, interrupt latency should be ____________
    (A) zero
    (B) minimal
    (C) maximum
    (D) dependent on the scheduling

22. The operating system keeps a small table containing information about all open files called ____________
    (A) file table
    (B) directory table
    (C) open-file table
    (D) system table

23. The operating system ________ the links when traversing directory trees, to preserve the acyclic structure of the system.
    (A) deletes
    (B) considers
    (C) ignores
    (D) none of the mentioned

24. To recover from failures in the network operations ____________ information may be maintained.
    (A) operating system
    (B) IP address
    (C) stateless
    (D) state

25. The two steps the operating system takes to use a disk to hold its files are ________ and ________
    (A) caching & logical formatting
    (B) logical formatting & swap space creation
    (C) swap space creation & caching
    (D) partitioning & logical formatting

—Darken Your Choice with HB Pencil—

1.	Ⓐ Ⓑ Ⓒ Ⓓ	6.	Ⓐ Ⓑ Ⓒ Ⓓ	11.	Ⓐ Ⓑ Ⓒ Ⓓ	16	Ⓐ Ⓑ Ⓒ Ⓓ	21.	Ⓐ Ⓑ Ⓒ Ⓓ
2.	Ⓐ Ⓑ Ⓒ Ⓓ	7.	Ⓐ Ⓑ Ⓒ Ⓓ	12.	Ⓐ Ⓑ Ⓒ Ⓓ	17.	Ⓐ Ⓑ Ⓒ Ⓓ	22.	Ⓐ Ⓑ Ⓒ Ⓓ
3.	Ⓐ Ⓑ Ⓒ Ⓓ	8.	Ⓐ Ⓑ Ⓒ Ⓓ	13.	Ⓐ Ⓑ Ⓒ Ⓓ	18.	Ⓐ Ⓑ Ⓒ Ⓓ	23.	Ⓐ Ⓑ Ⓒ Ⓓ
4.	Ⓐ Ⓑ Ⓒ Ⓓ	9.	Ⓐ Ⓑ Ⓒ Ⓓ	14.	Ⓐ Ⓑ Ⓒ Ⓓ	19.	Ⓐ Ⓑ Ⓒ Ⓓ	24.	Ⓐ Ⓑ Ⓒ Ⓓ
5.	Ⓐ Ⓑ Ⓒ Ⓓ	10.	Ⓐ Ⓑ Ⓒ Ⓓ	15.	Ⓐ Ⓑ Ⓒ Ⓓ	20.	Ⓐ Ⓑ Ⓒ Ⓓ	25.	Ⓐ Ⓑ Ⓒ Ⓓ

DATABASE MANAGEMENT SYSTEM

3

➤ Introduction to MS Access
➤ Working of MS Access

MULTIPLE CHOICE QUESTIONS

1. You can activate a cell by
   (A) Pressing the Tab key
   (B) Clicking the cell
   (C) Pressing an arrow key
   (D) All of these

2. Which of the following setup options can not be set in the page setup dialog box?
   (A) Printer selection
   (B) Vertical or horizontal placement
   (C) Orientation
   (D) Row and column titles

3. Which term refers to a specific set of values saved with the workbook?
   (A) Range
   (B) Scenario
   (C) Trend line
   (D) What-if analysis

4. You need the insert function dialog box. How do you get it?
   (A) Right click a cell and then click insert
   (B) Click the insert menu and then click function
   (C) Type = in a cell
   (D) All of these

5. Which of the following describes how to select all the cells in a single column?
   (A) Right click on column and select Pick from list
   (B) Use data – text to columns menu item
   (C) Left click on the gray column title button
   (D) Pressing Ctrl + A on the keyboard

6. When you use the fill effects in the format data series dialog box, you cannot
   (A) Rotate text on the chart
   (B) Select a fore ground color
   (C) Select a pattern
   (D) Select a background color

7. Paper spreadsheets can have all the same advantages as an electronic spreadsheet except which of the following?
   (A) Rows and columns
   (B) Headings
   (C) Speed
   (D) None

8. Which of the following is not a basic step in creating a worksheet?
   (A) Save the workbook
   (B) Modify the worksheet
   (C) Enter text and data
   (D) Copy the worksheet

9. What is a quick way to extend these numbers to a longer sequence, for instance 1 through 20?
   (A) Select both cells, and then drag the fill handle over the range you want, for instance 18 more rows.
   (B) Select the range you want, include both cells, point to fill on the Edit menu, and then click down.
   (C) Copy the second cell, click in the cell below it, on the standard toolbar click the down arrow on the Paste button, and then click Paste Special.
   (D) All of these

10. To insert three columns between columns D and E, you would
    (A) Select column D
    (B) Select column E
    (C) Select columns E, F and G
    (D) Select columns D, E, and F

11. To center worksheet titles across a range of cell, you must
    (A) Select the cells containing the title text and use the fill handle to center the text across a range of cells.
    (B) Widen the columns.
    (C) Select the cells containing the title text and use the fill handle to center the text across a range of cells.
    (D) Widen the column.

12. When integrating MS Word and Excel, the Word is usually the
    (A) Server
    (B) Source
    (C) Client
    (D) None

13. Charts tips can
    (A) Show the formatting of a data label
    (B) Show the name of a data series
    (C) Show the value of data point
    (D) Both (B) and (C)

14. The Name box
    (A) Shows location of the previously active cell
    (B) Appears at the left of the formula bar
    (C) Appears below the status bar
    (D) Appears below the menu bar

15. How do you change column width to fit the contents?
    (A) Single-click the boundary to the left to the column heading
    (B) Double click the boundary to the right of the column heading
    (C) Press Alt and single click anywhere in the column
    (D) All of these

16. When you work with large worksheets, you may need to:
    (A) Size the worksheet to fit on the specific number of pages
    (B) Add and remove page breaks
    (C) Specify only certain print areas
    (D) All of these

17. Hyperlinks cannot be
    (A) Special shapes like stars and banners
    (B) Drawing objects like rectangles ovals
    (C) Pictures
    (D) All can be hyperlinks

18. You can use the horizontal and vertical scroll bars to
    (A) Split a worksheet into two panes
    (B) View different rows and columns
    (C) Edit the contents of a cell
    (D) View different worksheets

19. What do we call a computer program that organizes data in rows and columns of cells? You might use this type of program to keep a record of the money you earned moving lawns over the summer.
    (A) Spreadsheet program
    (B) Database program
    (C) Word processor program
    (D) Desktop publisher program

20. You can add an image to a template by clicking the Insert Picture from File button on the _________ Toolbar.
    (A) Standard   (B) Formatting
    (C) Drawing   (D) Picture

21. What is the purpose of an index in MS Access?
    (A) To sort data in ascending or descending order
    (B) To create relationships between tables
    (C) To perform calculations on data
    (D) To improve the performance of database operations

22. Query design window has two parts. The upper part shows
    (A) Name of fields, field type and size
    (B) Sorting check boxes
    (C) Tables with fields and relationships between tables
    (D) None of these

23. In one-to-many relationship the table in 'one' side is called ________ and on 'many' side is called ________
    (A) Parent , Child
    (B) Child , Parent
    (C) Row , Column
    (D) None of these

24. To create relationship between two tables
    (A) drag any field from parent table and drop on child table
    (B) drag the foreign key of a table into the primary key of another table
    (C) drag the primary key of a table into foreign key of another table
    (D) None of these

25. Checkpoints are a part of
    (A) Recovery measures
    (B) Security measures
    (C) Concurrency measures
    (D) Authorization measures

Darken Your Choice with HB Pencil

1.	Ⓐ Ⓑ Ⓒ Ⓓ	6.	Ⓐ Ⓑ Ⓒ Ⓓ	11.	Ⓐ Ⓑ Ⓒ Ⓓ	16	Ⓐ Ⓑ Ⓒ Ⓓ	21.	Ⓐ Ⓑ Ⓒ Ⓓ
2.	Ⓐ Ⓑ Ⓒ Ⓓ	7.	Ⓐ Ⓑ Ⓒ Ⓓ	12.	Ⓐ Ⓑ Ⓒ Ⓓ	17.	Ⓐ Ⓑ Ⓒ Ⓓ	22.	Ⓐ Ⓑ Ⓒ Ⓓ
3.	Ⓐ Ⓑ Ⓒ Ⓓ	8.	Ⓐ Ⓑ Ⓒ Ⓓ	13.	Ⓐ Ⓑ Ⓒ Ⓓ	18.	Ⓐ Ⓑ Ⓒ Ⓓ	23.	Ⓐ Ⓑ Ⓒ Ⓓ
4.	Ⓐ Ⓑ Ⓒ Ⓓ	9.	Ⓐ Ⓑ Ⓒ Ⓓ	14.	Ⓐ Ⓑ Ⓒ Ⓓ	19.	Ⓐ Ⓑ Ⓒ Ⓓ	24.	Ⓐ Ⓑ Ⓒ Ⓓ
5.	Ⓐ Ⓑ Ⓒ Ⓓ	10.	Ⓐ Ⓑ Ⓒ Ⓓ	15.	Ⓐ Ⓑ Ⓒ Ⓓ	20.	Ⓐ Ⓑ Ⓒ Ⓓ	25.	Ⓐ Ⓑ Ⓒ Ⓓ

HTML AND CSS

LEARNING OBJECTIVES

➤ Basics of HTML
➤ Different HTML tags

MULTIPLE CHOICE QUESTIONS

1. How to define target in new page in HTML?

   (A) <a href = "http://www.navneetmehra.com/" target = "blank">Click Here</a>

   (B) <a href = "http://www.navneetmehra.com/" target = "_blank"> Click Here </a>

   (C) <a href = "http://www.navneetmehra.com/" target = "#blank"> Click Here </a>

   (D) <a href = "http://www.navneetmehra.com/" target = "@blank"> Click Here </a>

2. In HTML, Uniform Resource Identifier (URI) is used to

   (A) To create a frame document

   (B) To create an image map in the webpage

   (C) To customize the image in the webpage

   (D) To identify a name or a resource on the internet

3. CSS stands for

   (A) Cascading Style Sheet

   (B) Costume Style Sheet

   (C) Cascading System Style

   (D) None of these

4. What is the use of Web font in HTML?

   (A) This is the core font used to develop Web Pages.

   (B) This enables us to use fonts over the Web without installation.

   (C) This is the special font that developed by Microsoft Corporation.

   (D) All of these

5. What is <tt> tag in HTML?

   (A) It renders fonts as teletype text font style.

   (B) It renders fonts as truetype text font style.

   (C) It renders fonts as truncate text font style.

   (D) None of these

6. What is the use of Forms in HTML?

   (A) To display contents of email

   (B) To display animation effect

   (C) To collect user's input

   (D) None of these

7. What is the use of iframe in HTML?
   (A) To display a web page within a web page
   (B) To display a web page with animation effect
   (C) To display a web page without browser
   (D) All of these

8. Which HTML Tag is used to scroll a text in web page?
   (A) <marquee> ... </marquee>
   (B) <scroll> ... </scroll>
   (C) <round> ... </round>
   (D) <go> ... </go>

9. Which organization defines the Web Standards?
   (A) Microsoft Corporation
   (B) IBM Corporation
   (C) World Wide Web Consortium
   (D) Apple Inc.

10. How to set a picture as a background web page?
   (A) <body background= "backpic.gif">
   (B) <body background image= "backpic.gif">
   (C) <background= "backpic.gif">
   (D) <background image= "backpic.gif">

11. Which of following HTML Tag will insert a line break?
   (A) <p />
   (B) <lb />
   (C)
   (D) <break />

12. Which of the following tags are related to Table in HTML ?
   (A) <table> <row> <column>
   (B) <table> <tr> <td>
   (C) <table> <head> <body>
   (D) <table> <header> <footer>

13. Which of the following is correct HTML for inserting an image?
   (A) <image source="www. navneetmehra.com/ganesh.jpg" alt= "This is me" />
   (B) <img src= "www.navneetmehra. com/ganesh.jpg" alt= "This is me" />
   (C) <img source= "www.navneetmehra. com/ganesh.jpg" alt= "This is me" />
   (D) <img alt= "This is me">www. navneetmehra.com/ganesh.jpg</ img>

14. Choose the correct HTML tag to left-align the content of a cell.
   (A) <tdleft>
   (B) <td leftalign>
   (C) <td valign= "left">
   (D) <td align= "left">

15. Which tag is used to list the items with bullets?
   (A) <bullet>...</bullet>
   (B) <list>...</list>
   (C) <ul>...</ul>
   (D) <ol>...</ol>

16. Is it possible to insert a table within another table?
   (A) Yes, but there must be exactly 2 rows and 2 columns the in first table.
   (B) Yes, table can be inserted into cell of another table.
   (C) Yes, but there must be no border in the second table.
   (D) No, it's not possible.

17. What is the usage of alt value in <img> tag?
   (A) Alternative text for an Image
   (B) Alternative source of an Image
   (C) Caption of an Image
   (D) All of these

18. Which of the following is correct regarding meta tag in HTML?
   (A) <meta> ... </meta>
   (B) <meta name = " " />
   (C) <metadata> ... </metadata>
   (D) <metadata name = " " />

19. Which of the following is correct to set "Black" color as Background of page?
   (A) <body bgcolor = "#000000">
   (B) <body background = "#000000">
   (C) <body Background color = "#000000">
   (D) All of these

20. Which of the following is correct to align h1 tag to Right Alignment
   (A) <h1 align = "right"> ... </h1>
   (B) <h1 alignment = "right"> ... </h1>
   (C) <h1 tag align = "right"> ... </h1>
   (D) <h1 cannot make Right Alignment

21. Which of the following is correct to change font face in Web Page
   (A) <font = "font name"> ... </font>
   (B) <font name = "font name"> ... </font>
   (C) <font face = "font name"> ... </font>
   (D) Font Face cannot change

22. Which tag is used to display preformatted texts?
   (A) <pre> ... </ pre>
   (B) <prefor> ... </ prefor>
   (C) <pre text> ... </ pre text>
   (D) <pre format> ... </ pre format>

23. Which is the correct to create an Arabic numeral list
   (A) <ul type= "1">
   (B) <ol type= "1">
   (C) <il type= "1">
   (D) <li type= "1">

24. How to add alternative text for an Image?
   (A) <img src = "http://www.navneetmehra.com/logo.png" alternate = "Logo of website" />
   (B) <img src = "http://www.navneetmehra.com/logo.png" alt text = "Logo of website" />
   (C) <img src = "http://www.navneetmehra.com/logo.png" alternate text = "Logo of website" />
   (D) <img src = "http://www.navneetmehra.com/logo.png" alt = "Logo of website" />

25. How to embed Audio Files in HTML?
   (A) <embed src = "myfavsong.mid" width = "100" height = "15">
   (B) <embed sound = "myfavsong.mid" width = "100" height = "15">
   (C) <embed audio = "myfavsong.mid" width = "100" height = "15">
   (D) <embed music = "myfavsong.mid" width = "100" height = "15">

26. Which input attribute specifies that the input field should automatically get focused when the page loads?
    (A) Autofocus
    (B) Placeholder
    (C) Autocomplete
    (D) None of these

27. Meta attribute "Charset" has _______ value for Chinese characters.
    (A) UTF-8
    (B) Big5
    (C) euc-kr
    (D) None of these

28. The ID selector is written with the _______ character followed by the ID name.
    (A) Period   (B) Asterisks
    (C) Copyright   (D) Hash

29. _______ property helps to put the text fixed on the browser.
    (A) Static Positioning
    (B) Fixed Positioning
    (C) Relative Positioning
    (D) Absolute Positioning

30. The loop attribute of the video element indicates
    (A) That the browser should restart playback each time it reaches the end of the video.
    (B) That the video should begin playing immediately when the page is loaded.
    (C) That user control of playback should be blocked.
    (D) That the browser should download the video file when opening the web page.

---Darken Your Choice with HB Pencil---

1.	Ⓐ	Ⓑ	Ⓒ	Ⓓ	7.	Ⓐ	Ⓑ	Ⓒ	Ⓓ	13.	Ⓐ	Ⓑ	Ⓒ	Ⓓ	19	Ⓐ	Ⓑ	Ⓒ	Ⓓ	25.	Ⓐ	Ⓑ	Ⓒ	Ⓓ
2.	Ⓐ	Ⓑ	Ⓒ	Ⓓ	8.	Ⓐ	Ⓑ	Ⓒ	Ⓓ	14.	Ⓐ	Ⓑ	Ⓒ	Ⓓ	20.	Ⓐ	Ⓑ	Ⓒ	Ⓓ	26.	Ⓐ	Ⓑ	Ⓒ	Ⓓ
3.	Ⓐ	Ⓑ	Ⓒ	Ⓓ	9.	Ⓐ	Ⓑ	Ⓒ	Ⓓ	15.	Ⓐ	Ⓑ	Ⓒ	Ⓓ	21.	Ⓐ	Ⓑ	Ⓒ	Ⓓ	27.	Ⓐ	Ⓑ	Ⓒ	Ⓓ
4.	Ⓐ	Ⓑ	Ⓒ	Ⓓ	10.	Ⓐ	Ⓑ	Ⓒ	Ⓓ	16.	Ⓐ	Ⓑ	Ⓒ	Ⓓ	22.	Ⓐ	Ⓑ	Ⓒ	Ⓓ	28.	Ⓐ	Ⓑ	Ⓒ	Ⓓ
5.	Ⓐ	Ⓑ	Ⓒ	Ⓓ	11.	Ⓐ	Ⓑ	Ⓒ	Ⓓ	17.	Ⓐ	Ⓑ	Ⓒ	Ⓓ	23.	Ⓐ	Ⓑ	Ⓒ	Ⓓ	29.	Ⓐ	Ⓑ	Ⓒ	Ⓓ
6.	Ⓐ	Ⓑ	Ⓒ	Ⓓ	12.	Ⓐ	Ⓑ	Ⓒ	Ⓓ	18.	Ⓐ	Ⓑ	Ⓒ	Ⓓ	24.	Ⓐ	Ⓑ	Ⓒ	Ⓓ	30.	Ⓐ	Ⓑ	Ⓒ	Ⓓ

MS WORD

LEARNING OBJECTIVES

➤ Introduction to MS Word
➤ Working of MS Word

MULTIPLE CHOICE QUESTIONS

1. Which key do you press to force a page break?
   (A) CTRL + ALT
   (B) CTRL + Break
   (C) CTRL + Enter
   (D) None of these

2. Which menu do you choose to shade words and paragraph?
   (A) Format, borders and shading
   (B) Insert, borders and shading
   (C) View, shading
   (D) None of these

3. To view headers and footers, you must switch to
   (A) Normal view   (B) Print layout view
   (C) Print preview mode
   (D) Both (B) and (C)

4. Which of the following can you change using the page setup dialog box?
   (A) Margins
   (B) Page orientation
   (C) Vertical alignment
   (D) All of these

5. By default, your document prints with:
   (A) 1 inch top and bottom margins
   (B) A portrait orientation
   (C) 1.25 inches left and right margins
   (D) All of these

6. What happens when you insert an AutoShape by simply clicking in the document?
   (A) It appears near the insertion point
   (B) It is inserted in its default size
   (C) Is selected
   (D) All of these

7. What must be used to control the layering of objects?
   (A) Formatting toolbar
   (B) Picture toolbar
   (C) Drawing toolbar
   (D) Image toolbar

8. What is the shortcut key to "Center Align" the selected text?
   (A) Ctrl + C
   (B) Ctrl + E
   (C) Ctrl + F
   (D) None of these

9. What is the shortcut key to "Undo" the last action in a document?
   (A) Ctrl + X
   (B) Ctrl + Y
   (C) Ctrl + Z
   (D) None of these

10. What is the shortcut key to "Insert Hyperlink" in a document?
   (A) Ctrl + H
   (B) Ctrl + L
   (C) Ctrl + K
   (D) None of these

11. What is the shortcut key for "Find and Replace" dialog box?
   (A) Ctrl + F
   (B) Ctrl + R
   (C) Ctrl + H
   (D) Ctrl + Shift + F

12. What is the shortcut key for Spelling Check in document?
   (A) F7
   (B) Shift + F7
   (C) Ctrl + F7
   (D) Alt + F7

13. What is the shortcut key to Update Formula in a table?
   (A) F9
   (B) Alt + F9
   (C) Ctrl + F9
   (D) Shift + F9

14. What is the shortcut key to close Active Document in Microsoft Word?
   (A) Ctrl + F4
   (B) Shift + F4
   (C) Ctrl + Shift + F4
   (D) None of these

15. What is the shortcut key for "Font" dialog box?
   (A) Ctrl + F
   (B) Ctrl + D
   (C) Ctrl + G
   (D) None of these

16. What is the shortcut key for 'Superscripting' the selected text?
   (A) Ctrl + =   (B) Ctrl + –
   (C) Ctrl + Shift +   (D) Ctrl + Shift + –

17. What is the shortcut key for 'Subscripting' the selected text?
   (A) Ctrl + =
   (B) Ctrl + –
   (C) Ctrl + Shift + =
   (D) Ctrl + Shift + –

18. Ctrl + A
   (A) Aligns Right
   (B) Selects All
   (C) Changes font
   (D) Saves document

19. Ctrl + B
   (A) Searches the selected text
   (B) Pastes the selected text
   (C) Makes the selected text bold
   (D) Opens the specified file

20. Ctrl + C
   (A) Copies the selected text
   (B) Cuts the selected text
   (C) Prints the selected text
   (D) Pastes the selected text

21. Ctrl + D
   (A) Deletes Dialog Box
   (B) Font Dialog Box
   (C) Deletes All
   (D) Does nothing

22. Ctrl + E
   (A) Exits Application
   (B) Selects All
   (C) Clears All
   (D) Aligns Center

23. Ctrl + F
   (A) Opens Find and Replace Dialog box with activating Find Tab
   (B) Opens Page Setup Dialog box with activating Layout Tab

(C) Opens Font Dialog Box with activating Font tab

(D) Opens File Save as Dialog box

24. Ctrl + H

(A) Opens Find and Replace Dialog box with activating Replace Tab.

(B) Opens Format Dialog box activating Insert Hyper Link tab.

(C) Opens Insert Dialog box activating Insert Hyper Link Tab.

(D) Opens Insert Hyper Link Dialog box.

25. Ctrl + I

(A) Italic

(B) Left Indent

(C) Saves Document

(D) Close Document

26. Ctrl + J

(A) Aligns Justify

(B) Inserts Hyperlink

(c) Searches a document

(D) Prints a document

27. What is the use of bookmarks in Microsoft Word?

(A) To easily correct the spelling errors.

(B) To quickly jump to a specific location in the document.

(C) To quickly jump to the ending of the document.

(D) To create a link within the document.

28. What is the shortcut-key for manual line break?

(A) CTRL + Enter

(B) Alt + Enter

(C) Shift + Enter

(D) Space + Enter

29. Which feature helps you to insert contents of the Clipboard as text without any formatting?

(A) Paste Special

(B) Format Painter

(C) Page Setup

(D) Styles

30. Which feature is used to replace straight quotes with smart quotes as you type?

(A) Auto Correct as you type

(B) Auto Change as you type

(C) Auto Format as you type

(D) Smart Tags as you type

HOTS (ACHIEVERS SECTION)

31. Switching between portrait and landscape modes involves the:

(A) Header and footer toolbar

(B) Print layout view

(C) Page setup dialog box

(D) None of these

32. Triple Click

(A) Opens Paragraph Dialog box activating Go To Tab

(B) Selects line or paragraph of the text the mouse triple-clicked.

(C) Opens Find and Replace Dialog box with activating Go To Tab

(D) Opens Go To Dialog box

33. How will MS Word respond in repeated word?

(A) A Red wavy line under the repeated word

(B) A Green wavy line under the repeated word

(C) A Blue wavy line under the repeated word

(D) None of these

34. Tabs stop position cannot be the following alignment
    (A) Decimal Alignment
    (B) Center Alignment
    (C) Bar Alignment
    (D) Justify Alignment
35. How to use Format Painter multiple times?
    (A) By Clicking on Lock Format Painter Icon
    (B) By Double Clicking on the Format Painter Icon
    (C) By Selecting Edit → Format Painter → Multiple Use
    (D) Format Painter cannot be used multiple times

──────Darken Your Choice with HB Pencil──────

1.	Ⓐ Ⓑ Ⓒ Ⓓ	8.	Ⓐ Ⓑ Ⓒ Ⓓ	15.	Ⓐ Ⓑ Ⓒ Ⓓ	22	Ⓐ Ⓑ Ⓒ Ⓓ	29.	Ⓐ Ⓑ Ⓒ Ⓓ
2.	Ⓐ Ⓑ Ⓒ Ⓓ	9.	Ⓐ Ⓑ Ⓒ Ⓓ	16.	Ⓐ Ⓑ Ⓒ Ⓓ	23.	Ⓐ Ⓑ Ⓒ Ⓓ	30.	Ⓐ Ⓑ Ⓒ Ⓓ
3.	Ⓐ Ⓑ Ⓒ Ⓓ	10.	Ⓐ Ⓑ Ⓒ Ⓓ	17.	Ⓐ Ⓑ Ⓒ Ⓓ	24.	Ⓐ Ⓑ Ⓒ Ⓓ	31.	Ⓐ Ⓑ Ⓒ Ⓓ
4.	Ⓐ Ⓑ Ⓒ Ⓓ	11.	Ⓐ Ⓑ Ⓒ Ⓓ	18.	Ⓐ Ⓑ Ⓒ Ⓓ	25.	Ⓐ Ⓑ Ⓒ Ⓓ	32.	Ⓐ Ⓑ Ⓒ Ⓓ
5.	Ⓐ Ⓑ Ⓒ Ⓓ	12.	Ⓐ Ⓑ Ⓒ Ⓓ	19.	Ⓐ Ⓑ Ⓒ Ⓓ	26.	Ⓐ Ⓑ Ⓒ Ⓓ	33.	Ⓐ Ⓑ Ⓒ Ⓓ
6.	Ⓐ Ⓑ Ⓒ Ⓓ	13.	Ⓐ Ⓑ Ⓒ Ⓓ	20.	Ⓐ Ⓑ Ⓒ Ⓓ	27.	Ⓐ Ⓑ Ⓒ Ⓓ	34.	Ⓐ Ⓑ Ⓒ Ⓓ
7.	Ⓐ Ⓑ Ⓒ Ⓓ	14.	Ⓐ Ⓑ Ⓒ Ⓓ	21.	Ⓐ Ⓑ Ⓒ Ⓓ	28.	Ⓐ Ⓑ Ⓒ Ⓓ	35.	Ⓐ Ⓑ Ⓒ Ⓓ

MS POWERPOINT

LEARNING OBJECTIVES

➤ Introduction to MS PowerPoint
➤ Working of MS PowerPoint

MULTIPLE CHOICE QUESTIONS

1. Material consisting of text and numbers is best represented as
   (A) A table slide   (B) A bullet slide
   (C) A title slide   (D) All of these

2. Which of the following gets displayed when an image is selected?
   (A) Add clip art only if it relates to your topic
   (B) Be sure to place at least one clipart image per slide
   (C) Resize the image so as it takes up as much space as your text
   (D) Both (A) and (B)

3. The Microsoft clip gallery allows you to
   (A) Add word art images to a slide
   (B) Spell check your presentation
   (C) Add clip art images to a slide or slides
   (D) Add slides to a presentation

4. Which command selects all objects at one time when selecting multiple objects to be deleted?
   (A) Alt + A
   (B) Ctrl + A
   (C) Shift + Enter
   (D) Edit, Select All

5. Auto clip art is a feature that
   (A) Automatically places clip art in your presentation
   (B) Scans your presentation for incorrect spelling of words on each slide
   (C) Scans your presentation for incorrect spelling in word art objects
   (D) All of these

6. To select all the boxes of an organization chart,
   (A) Click edit, select all
   (B) Right click the chart background, click select all
   (C) Press and hold the shift key and click each box
   (D) All of these

7. To adjust the width of table columns, you
   (A) Click table menu. Column width, then make adjustments
   (B) Drag the vertical gridline between two columns
   (C) Drag the column markers on the table ruler bar
   (D) Both (B) and (C)

8. To add a new row to a table, you would
   (A) Click the insert rows command on the insert menu
   (B) Press the enter key
   (C) Click the insert rows button on the standard toolbar
   (D) None of these

9. After moving a clip art image to a particular location on the slide, you can immediately reverse the action using the
   (A) Click the not do move object command on the edit menu
   (B) Click on the undo button
   (C) Click on the redo button
   (D) All of these

10. You can edit an embedded organization chart object by
   (A) Clicking the edit object
   (B) Double clicking the organization chart object
   (C) Right clicking the chart object, then clicking edit MS-Organization Chart object
   (D) Both (B) and (C)

11. You edit an embedded table object by
   (A) Clicking the edit sub command of the document object command on the edit menu
   (B) Double clicking the table object
   (C) Right clicking the table object, then clicking edit document on the edit menu
   (D) All of these

12. You can embed a Microsoft Word table in a slide by
   (A) Clicking the insert new slide button on the standard toolbar, then double clicking table.
   (B) Clicking the insert Microsoft word table button on the formatting toolbar.
   (C) Clicking the insert Microsoft word table button on the standard toolbar.
   (D) Both (A) and (C)

13. What is the name of the form used to input chart values?
   (A) Datasheet   (B) Microsoft Excel
   (C) Microsoft graph (D) Auto form

14. Which of the following you must complete first in order to delete an object?
   (A) Double click the image
   (B) Select the image
   (C) Resize the image
   (D) Move the image to a new location

15. What is the term used to describe the separation of a clip art object into different parts so that it becomes a PowerPoint object?
   (A) Embedding   (B) Regrouping
   (C) Ungrouping   (D) Grouping

16. The auto shapes tool provides you with
   (A) Fancy text to place on your slide
   (B) Commonly found shapes
   (C) Any shape you want to add on a slide
   (D) Clip art that is related to your presentation

17. Which of the following should be used when you want to add a slide to an existing presentation?
   (A) File → add a new slide
   (B) Insert → new slide
   (C) File → open
   (D) File → new

18. An organization has a president, vice president, managers and supervisors. On what level of an organization chart is the vice president?
   (A) Fourth level   (B) Third level
   (C) Second level   (D) First level

19. Which of the following includes special effects that can be applied to drawing objects?
   (A) Gradient fills
   (B) Line color and style
   (C) Rotating
   (D) All of these

20. What is the term used when a clip art image changes the direction it faces?
    (A) Group
    (B) Flip
    (C) Rotate
    (D) Both (B) and (C)

21. What is the term used when you press and hold the left mouse key and move the mouse around the slide?
    (A) Highlighting
    (B) Dragging
    (C) Selecting
    (D) Both (B) and (C)

22. The size of a table object
    (A) Is dependent on the amount of text within the table
    (B) Is determined by the presentation design but can be changed
    (C) Is determined by the presentation design and cannot be changed
    (D) Both (A) and (C)

23. The size of an organization chart object
    (A) Is determined by the presentation design and cannot be changed
    (B) Is determined by the presentation design but can be changed in PowerPoint
    (C) Is dependent on the amount of text within the organization chart
    (D) Both (B) and (C)

24. Which of the following format options should be used to display dollars on an axis?
    (A) Normal
    (B) Percentage
    (C) Currency
    (D) Comma

25. To maintain the perspective (height and width ratio) of an object when resizing, you need to
    (A) Press and hold the shift key while dragging a corner sizing handle.
    (B) Press and hold the alt + ctrl keys while dragging a middle handle.
    (C) Drag the corner sizing handle.
    (D) Both (A) and (C)

26. Which of the following is/are true about rulers and guides?
    (A) Rulers and guides can be turned on or off.
    (B) Rulers and guides print on the slide.
    (C) Rulers and guides help place objects on the slide.
    (D) Both (A) and (C)

27. Which of the following options changes the fill color of an object back to the default color?
    (A) Template
    (B) Automatic
    (C) Patterns
    (D) Fill colors

28. Which of the following should you use to add shading to a drawing object on or an auto shape object?
    (A) Text box tool
    (B) Line tool
    (C) Fill color
    (D) Both (B) and (C)

29. Which of the following tools enable you to add text to a slide without using the standard place holders?
    (A) Text box tool
    (B) Line tool
    (C) Fill color
    (D) Auto shapes tool

30. A cell is defined as
    (A) The intersection of a column and a row
    (B) An input box
    (C) A rectangular marker
    (D) All of these

31. You can embed an organization chart in a slide by
    (A) Clicking the object command on the edit menu
    (B) Clicking the insert new slide button on the standard toolbar, then double clicking the organization chart auto layout
    (C) Clicking the MS organization chart button on the formatting toolbar
    (D) Clicking the MS organization chart button on the standard toolbar

32. You can add multiple subordinates to a position by
    (A) Clicking the subordinate button as you press and hold shift
    (B) Clicking the subordinate button each and every time you add a subordinate
    (C) Clicking the subordinate button as many times as the desired boxes
    (D) All of these

33. To edit the text within the boxes of an organization chart, you
    (A) Select the box and text, then make the changes.
    (B) Select the box, then make the changes.
    (C) Highlight the text, then make the changes.
    (D) Highlight the box, then make the changes.

34. Which of the following best describes serifs?
    (A) Serifs help to differentiate between similar looking letters.
    (B) Serifs fonts are best for viewing test at a distance.
    (C) Serifs are fine cross strokes that appear at the bottom and top of a letter.
    (D) Serif fonts are very simple in appearance.

35. What will happen if you release the mouse button before releasing the shift key when you draw a square?
    (A) The square will not be a perfect square.
    (B) The square will not be at the center of the slide.
    (C) The square will be smaller.
    (D) The square will be larger.

Darken Your Choice with HB Pencil

1.	Ⓐ Ⓑ Ⓒ Ⓓ	8.	Ⓐ Ⓑ Ⓒ Ⓓ	15.	Ⓐ Ⓑ Ⓒ Ⓓ	22	Ⓐ Ⓑ Ⓒ Ⓓ	29.	Ⓐ Ⓑ Ⓒ Ⓓ
2.	Ⓐ Ⓑ Ⓒ Ⓓ	9.	Ⓐ Ⓑ Ⓒ Ⓓ	16.	Ⓐ Ⓑ Ⓒ Ⓓ	23.	Ⓐ Ⓑ Ⓒ Ⓓ	30.	Ⓐ Ⓑ Ⓒ Ⓓ
3.	Ⓐ Ⓑ Ⓒ Ⓓ	10.	Ⓐ Ⓑ Ⓒ Ⓓ	17.	Ⓐ Ⓑ Ⓒ Ⓓ	24.	Ⓐ Ⓑ Ⓒ Ⓓ	31.	Ⓐ Ⓑ Ⓒ Ⓓ
4.	Ⓐ Ⓑ Ⓒ Ⓓ	11.	Ⓐ Ⓑ Ⓒ Ⓓ	18.	Ⓐ Ⓑ Ⓒ Ⓓ	25.	Ⓐ Ⓑ Ⓒ Ⓓ	32.	Ⓐ Ⓑ Ⓒ Ⓓ
5.	Ⓐ Ⓑ Ⓒ Ⓓ	12.	Ⓐ Ⓑ Ⓒ Ⓓ	19.	Ⓐ Ⓑ Ⓒ Ⓓ	26.	Ⓐ Ⓑ Ⓒ Ⓓ	33.	Ⓐ Ⓑ Ⓒ Ⓓ
6.	Ⓐ Ⓑ Ⓒ Ⓓ	13.	Ⓐ Ⓑ Ⓒ Ⓓ	20.	Ⓐ Ⓑ Ⓒ Ⓓ	27.	Ⓐ Ⓑ Ⓒ Ⓓ	34.	Ⓐ Ⓑ Ⓒ Ⓓ
7.	Ⓐ Ⓑ Ⓒ Ⓓ	14.	Ⓐ Ⓑ Ⓒ Ⓓ	21.	Ⓐ Ⓑ Ⓒ Ⓓ	28.	Ⓐ Ⓑ Ⓒ Ⓓ	35.	Ⓐ Ⓑ Ⓒ Ⓓ

MS EXCEL

LEARNING OBJECTIVES

➤ Introduction to MS Excel
➤ Working of MS Excel

MULTIPLE CHOICE QUESTIONS

1. What is the AutoComplete feature of Excel?
   (A) It automatically completes abbreviated words.
   (B) It completes text entries that match an existing entry in the same column.
   (C) It completes text and numeric entries that match an existing entry in the same column.
   (D) It completes text entries that match an existing entry in the same worksheet.

2. Which of the following is correct?
   (A) =AVERAGE(4, 5, 6, 7)
   (B) =AVERAGE(A1, B1, C1)
   (C) =AVERAGE(A1:A9, B1:B9)
   (D) =All of these

3. Which of the following functions will return a value of 8?
   (A) ROUNDUP(8.4999, 0)
   (B) ROUNDDOWN(8.4999, 0)
   (C) ROUND(8.4999, 0)
   (D) Only (B) and (C)

4. How to restrict to run a macro automatically when starting Microsoft Excel?
   (A) Hold down the SHIFT key during startup.
   (B) Hold down the CTRL key during startup.
   (C) Hold down the ESC key during startup.
   (D) Hold down the ALT key during startup.

5. How to remove the unwanted action from recorded macro without recording the whole macro again?
   (A) By using the Find and Edit Action Option
   (B) By clicking on the Refresh button in the Macro toolbar
   (C) By editing the macro in the Visual Basic Editor
   (D) Macro cannot be edited

6. What should be added before a fraction to avoid entering it as a date?
   (A) //
   (B) FR
   (C) Zero
   (D) Zero Space

7. Which of the following functions will use to find the highest number in a series of number?
   (A) MAX(B1:B3)
   (B) MAXIMUM (B1:B3)
   (C) HIGH (B1:B3)
   (D) HIGHEST(B1:B3)

8. What does the NOW() function return?
   (A) It returns the serial number of the current date and time.
   (B) It returns the serial number of the current date.
   (C) It returns the serial number of the current time.
   (D) None of these

9. What value will be displayed if the formula = "$55.00" + 5 is entered into a cell?
   (A) $60
   (B) 60
   (C) "$55.00" + 5
   (D) $60.00

10. What is the shortcut key to insert current date in a cell?
    (A) CTRL + D
    (B) CTRL + T
    (C) CTRL + ;
    (D) CTRL + /

11. Which of the following syntax is correct regarding to SUM function in Excel?
    (A) =SUM (A1, B1)
    (B) =SUM (A1:B9)
    (C) =SUM (A1:A9, B1:B9)
    (D) All of these

12. What is the shortcut key to hide entire column?
    (A) CTRL + –
    (B) CTRL + 0
    (C) CTRL + H
    (D) CTRL + C

13. How to specify cell range from A9 to A99 in Excel?
    (A) (A9, A99)
    (B) (A9 to A99)
    (C) (A9 : A99)
    (D) (A9 – A99)

14. Clear the contents by pressing "DELETE" key from a keyboard will clear
    (A) Text Only
    (B) Format Only
    (C) Contents Only
    (D) Both Contents and Format

15. Which of the following shortcuts can be used to insert a new line in the same cell?
    (A) Enter
    (B) Alt + Enter
    (C) Ctrl + Enter
    (D) Shift + Enter

16. A smart tag will be removed from a cell when
    (A) the cell is moved
    (B) the cell is hidden
    (C) the data in the cell is changed or deleted
    (D) the formatting of the cell is changed

17. Which of the following is correct?
    (A) =POWER(2^3)
    (B) =POWER(2,3)
    (C) =POWER(2#3)
    (D) =POWER(2*3)

18. Selecting the Rows 5 and 6, then choosing Insert → Row. What will happen?
    (A) 2 Rows will be inserted after Row 4.
    (B) 2 Rows will be inserted after Row 5.
    (C) 2 Rows will be inserted after Row 6.
    (D) 2 Rows will be inserted after Row 7.

19. If 4/6 entered in a cell without applying any formats, Excel will treat this as

(A) Fraction   (B) Number

(C) Text   (D) Date

20. If the values in A1 is "MCQ" and B1 is "Questions", which function will return "MCQ@Questions" in cell C1?

(A) =A1 + "@" + B1

(B) =A1 # "@" # B1

(C) =A1 & "@" & B1

(D) =A1 $ "@" $ B1

21. How to fit long texts in a single cell with multiple lines?

(A) Start typing in the cell and press the Enter key to start another line.

(B) Use the Wrap Text option in the Format → Alignment menu.

(C) Use the Shrink to Fit option in the Format → Cells → Alignment menu.

(D) All of these

22. If a particular workbook has to be opened each time Excel started, where should the workbook be placed?

(A) AUTOEXEC Folder

(B) AUTOSTART Folder

(C) EXCELSTART Folder

(D) XLSTART Folder

23. If the cell B1 contains the formula = A1, which of the following statements is true

(A) There is a relative reference to cell A1

(B) There is an absolute reference to cell A1

(C) Further changes in value of A1 will not affect the value of B1

(D) Further changes in value of B1 will affect the value of A1

24. Worksheet can be renamed by

(A) Adding ? symbol at the end of filename while saving workbook.

(B) Click on Worksheet tab by Holding CTRL Key and type new name.

(C) Double Click on the Worksheet tab and type new name.

(D) Worksheet cannot be renamed.

25. What is the shortcut key to hide the entire row?

(A) CTRL + H

(B) CTRL + R

(C) CTRL + 9

(D) CTRL + –

26. What is the shortcut key to insert a new comment in a cell?

(A) F2

(B) Alt + F2

(C) Ctrl + F2

(D) Shift + F2

27. Which option allows you to Bold all the negative values within the selected cell range:

(A) Zero Formatting

(B) Conditional Formatting

(C) Compare Formatting

(D) Negative Formatting

28. What is the shortcut key to insert new sheet in current workbook?

(A) F11

(B) Alt + F11

(C) Ctrl + F11

(D) Shift + F11

29. Which one is the last column header in Excel?

(A) XFD

(B) XFX

(C) XFL

(D) XFT

30. In maximum, how many sheets can be set as default while creating new workbook?

(A) 254

(B) 255

(C) 256

(D) No Limit

31. Selecting the Column G and H then choosing Insert → Columns. What will happen?
    (A) 2 Columns will be inserted after Column F.
    (B) 2 Columns will be inserted after Column G.
    (C) 2 Columns will be inserted after Column H.
    (D) 2 Columns will be inserted after Column I.

32. How to restrict the values of a cell so that only whole numbers between 9 and 99 can be entered in a cell?
    (A) The Settings tab under the menu Format → Cells.
    (B) The Settings tab under the menu Data → Validation.
    (C) The Settings tab under the menu Data → Filter → Advanced Filter.
    (D) the Settings tab under the menu Format → Conditional Formatting.

33. What is the quickest way to select the entire worksheet?
    (A) Choose Edit → Select all from the Menu

(B) Click on the first column, press Ctrl, and then click on the last column.
(C) Click on the first column, press Shift, and then click on the last column.
(D) Click on the rectangle box on the upper left corner where column headings and row headings meet.

34. Which of the following options is appropriate to show the numbers 9779851089510 in a cell?
    (A) Enclose the number in brackets.
    (B) Place the character T before the number.
    (C) Place the character TX before the number.
    (D) Apply the Text format in the cell and type the numbers.

35. Which of the following is correct syntax in Excel?
    (A) =IF(LogicalTest, TrueResult, FalseResult)
    (B) =IF(LogicalTest, (TrueResult, FalseResult)
    (C) =IF(LogicalTest, TrueResult) (LogicalTest, FalseResult)
    (D) =IF(LogicalTest, TrueResult), IF (LogicalTest, FalseResult)

—Darken Your Choice with HB Pencil—

	A B C D		A B C D		A B C D		A B C D		A B C D
1.	Ⓐ Ⓑ Ⓒ Ⓓ	8.	Ⓐ Ⓑ Ⓒ Ⓓ	15.	Ⓐ Ⓑ Ⓒ Ⓓ	22	Ⓐ Ⓑ Ⓒ Ⓓ	29.	Ⓐ Ⓑ Ⓒ Ⓓ
2.	Ⓐ Ⓑ Ⓒ Ⓓ	9.	Ⓐ Ⓑ Ⓒ Ⓓ	16.	Ⓐ Ⓑ Ⓒ Ⓓ	23.	Ⓐ Ⓑ Ⓒ Ⓓ	30.	Ⓐ Ⓑ Ⓒ Ⓓ
3.	Ⓐ Ⓑ Ⓒ Ⓓ	10.	Ⓐ Ⓑ Ⓒ Ⓓ	17.	Ⓐ Ⓑ Ⓒ Ⓓ	24.	Ⓐ Ⓑ Ⓒ Ⓓ	31.	Ⓐ Ⓑ Ⓒ Ⓓ
4.	Ⓐ Ⓑ Ⓒ Ⓓ	11.	Ⓐ Ⓑ Ⓒ Ⓓ	18.	Ⓐ Ⓑ Ⓒ Ⓓ	25.	Ⓐ Ⓑ Ⓒ Ⓓ	32.	Ⓐ Ⓑ Ⓒ Ⓓ
5.	Ⓐ Ⓑ Ⓒ Ⓓ	12.	Ⓐ Ⓑ Ⓒ Ⓓ	19.	Ⓐ Ⓑ Ⓒ Ⓓ	26.	Ⓐ Ⓑ Ⓒ Ⓓ	33.	Ⓐ Ⓑ Ⓒ Ⓓ
6.	Ⓐ Ⓑ Ⓒ Ⓓ	13.	Ⓐ Ⓑ Ⓒ Ⓓ	20.	Ⓐ Ⓑ Ⓒ Ⓓ	27.	Ⓐ Ⓑ Ⓒ Ⓓ	34.	Ⓐ Ⓑ Ⓒ Ⓓ
7.	Ⓐ Ⓑ Ⓒ Ⓓ	14.	Ⓐ Ⓑ Ⓒ Ⓓ	21.	Ⓐ Ⓑ Ⓒ Ⓓ	28.	Ⓐ Ⓑ Ⓒ Ⓓ	35.	Ⓐ Ⓑ Ⓒ Ⓓ

INTERNET AND VIRUSES

LEARNING OBJECTIVES

➤ Basics of Internet
➤ Web browsers
➤ E-mail

MULTIPLE CHOICE QUESTIONS

1. Which protocol is used to report error message?
   (A) TCP
   (B) IP
   (C) ICMP
   (D) SMTP

2. Which is not the application level protocol?
   (A) FTP
   (B) S/MIME
   (C) PGP
   (D) HTTP

3. Which is the false statement?
   (A) Telnet is used for remote login.
   (B) FTP can transfer files between two hosts.
   (C) TFTP rely on TCP.
   (D) SMTP used to send mail message.

4. URL stands for:
   (A) Universal Resource Locator
   (B) Uniform Resource Locator
   (C) Uniform Radio Locator
   (D) None of these

5. Which is not the server side programming language?
   (A) JSP
   (B) ASP
   (C) JavaScript
   (D) PHP

6. FTP can be run on:
   (A) Unix
   (B) Linux
   (C) Dos/Windows
   (D) All of these

7. In HTTPS 'S' stands for:
   (A) Simple
   (B) Secured
   (C) Server
   (D) None of these

8. Which is not the requirement of the internet?
   (A) Operating System
   (B) Dos
   (C) Web browser
   (D) Modem

9. Which protocol is used for browsing website?
   (A) TCP
   (B) HTTP
   (C) FTP
   (D) TFTP

10. Which is not a browser?
    (A) Internet Explorer
    (B) Opera
    (C) Mozilla
    (D) Google

11. Which is not a search engine?
    (A) Altavista.com
    (B) Google.com
    (C) Facebook.com
    (D) Yahoo.com
12. Email stands for:
    (A) Easy mail
    (B) Electronic mail
    (C) Electric mail
    (D) None of these
13. Which is the chatting application?
    (A) WhatsApp
    (B) Google earth
    (C) Youtube
    (D) None of these
14. Which service provides 3D view of earth?
    (A) Google Earth
    (B) Wikipedia
    (C) Skype
    (D) None of these
15. Which is the threat for clients?
    (A) Virus
    (B) Worms
    (C) Trojan Horse
    (D) All of these
16. Which is not the application of internet?
    (A) Communication
    (B) Banking
    (C) Shopping
    (D) Sleeping
17. Which is the advantage of e-business?
    (A) Better Service
    (B) Reduction of cost
    (C) Reduction of paper work
    (D) All of these
18. What is the difference between the Internet and an intranet?
    (A) One is public, the other is private
    (B) One is safer than the other
    (C) One can be monitored, the other can't
    (D) None of these
19. What kind of data can you send by e-mail?
    (A) Audio
    (B) Pictures
    (C) Video
    (D) All of these
20. Which of these is a search engine?
    (A) FTP
    (B) Google
    (C) Archie
    (D) ARPANET
21. How do you subscribe to an Internet mailing list?
    (A) Contact your Internet service provider
    (B) Send e-mail to the list manager
    (C) Telephone the mailing list webmaster
    (D) Send a letter to the list
22. What is a web browser?
    (A) A kind of spider
    (B) A computer that stores WWW files
    (C) A person who likes to look at websites
    (D) A software program that allows you to access sites on the World Wide Web
23. Which of these is an e-mail address?
    (A) Professor.at.learnthenet
    (B) Www.learnthenet.com
    (C) Professor@learnthenet.com
    (D) Professor@learnthenet
24. http://www.classzone.com is an example of
    (A) A URL
    (B) An access code
    (C) A directory
    (D) A server

25. What are the three main search expressions, or operators, recognized by Boolean logic?
   (A) FROM, TO, WHOM
   (B) AND, OR, NOT
   (C) SEARCH, KEYWORD, TEXT
   (D) AND, OR, BUT

26. What is a URL?
   (A) A computer software program
   (B) A type of UFO
   (C) The address of a document or "page" on the World Wide Web
   (D) An acronym for Uniform Resources Learning

27. Which one of the following is a search engine?
   (A) Macromedia Flash
   (B) Google
   (C) Netscape
   (D) Librarians' Index to the Internet

28. Internet is
   (A) A local computer network
   (B) A world wide network of computers
   (C) An interconnected network of computers
   (D) A world wide interconnected network of computers which use a common protocol to communicate with one another

29. The facilities available on the internet are
   (i) Electronic mail
   (ii) Remote login
   (iii) File transfer
   (iv) Word processing
   (A) i, ii
   (B) i, ii, iii
   (C) i, ii, iv
   (D) ii, iii and iv

30. Internet requires:
   (A) An international agreement to connect computers
   (B) A local area network
   (C) A commonly agreed set of rules to communicate between computers
   (D) A World Wide Web

HOTS (ACHIEVERS SECTION)

31. Internet addresses must always have at least
   (i) A country name or organization type
   (ii) Internet service provider's name
   (iii) Name of organization
   (iv) Name of individual
   (v) Type of organization
   (A) i, ii, iii   (B) ii, iii, iv
   (C) i, iii   (D) ii, iii, iv, v

32. Internet packet data structure consists of
   (i) Source address
   (ii) Destination address
   (iii) Serial number of packets
   (iv) Message bytes
   (v) Control bits for error checking
   (vi) Path identification bits
   (A) i, ii, iii
   (B) i, ii, iii, iv
   (C) i, ii, iii, iv, v
   (D) i, ii, iii, iv, v, vi

33. The time taken by internet packets
   (A) Can be predetermined before transmission
   (B) May be different for different packets
   (C) Is irrelevant for audio packets
   (D) None of these

34. By an extranet, we mean
    (A) An extra fast computer network
    (B) The intranets of two co-operating organizations interconnected via a secure leased line
    (C) An extra network used by an organization for higher reliability
    (D) An extra connection to internet provided to co-operating organization

35. Which of the following statement is not correct about IP address?

    (A) IP address is always unique for each computer.
    (B) An IP address consists of four bytes (or 32 bits) each of which can be a number from 0 to 255.
    (C) For browsing or sending an email, an IP address assigned to the computer is required.
    (D) All are correct

1.	Ⓐ Ⓑ Ⓒ Ⓓ	8.	Ⓐ Ⓑ Ⓒ Ⓓ	15.	Ⓐ Ⓑ Ⓒ Ⓓ	22	Ⓐ Ⓑ Ⓒ Ⓓ	29.	Ⓐ Ⓑ Ⓒ Ⓓ
2.	Ⓐ Ⓑ Ⓒ Ⓓ	9.	Ⓐ Ⓑ Ⓒ Ⓓ	16.	Ⓐ Ⓑ Ⓒ Ⓓ	23.	Ⓐ Ⓑ Ⓒ Ⓓ	30.	Ⓐ Ⓑ Ⓒ Ⓓ
3.	Ⓐ Ⓑ Ⓒ Ⓓ	10.	Ⓐ Ⓑ Ⓒ Ⓓ	17.	Ⓐ Ⓑ Ⓒ Ⓓ	24.	Ⓐ Ⓑ Ⓒ Ⓓ	31.	Ⓐ Ⓑ Ⓒ Ⓓ
4.	Ⓐ Ⓑ Ⓒ Ⓓ	11.	Ⓐ Ⓑ Ⓒ Ⓓ	18.	Ⓐ Ⓑ Ⓒ Ⓓ	25.	Ⓐ Ⓑ Ⓒ Ⓓ	32.	Ⓐ Ⓑ Ⓒ Ⓓ
5.	Ⓐ Ⓑ Ⓒ Ⓓ	12.	Ⓐ Ⓑ Ⓒ Ⓓ	19.	Ⓐ Ⓑ Ⓒ Ⓓ	26.	Ⓐ Ⓑ Ⓒ Ⓓ	33.	Ⓐ Ⓑ Ⓒ Ⓓ
6.	Ⓐ Ⓑ Ⓒ Ⓓ	13.	Ⓐ Ⓑ Ⓒ Ⓓ	20.	Ⓐ Ⓑ Ⓒ Ⓓ	27.	Ⓐ Ⓑ Ⓒ Ⓓ	34.	Ⓐ Ⓑ Ⓒ Ⓓ
7.	Ⓐ Ⓑ Ⓒ Ⓓ	14.	Ⓐ Ⓑ Ⓒ Ⓓ	21.	Ⓐ Ⓑ Ⓒ Ⓓ	28.	Ⓐ Ⓑ Ⓒ Ⓓ	35.	Ⓐ Ⓑ Ⓒ Ⓓ

NETWORKING AND MULTIMEDIA

LEARNING OBJECTIVES

➤ Basic of Network
➤ Types of network

MULTIPLE CHOICE QUESTIONS

1. In the mesh topology, relationship between one device and another is ________.
   (A) Primary to peer
   (B) Peer to primary
   (C) Primary to secondary
   (D) Peer to Peer

2. The performance of data communications network depends on ________.
   (A) Number of users
   (B) The hardware and software
   (C) The transmission
   (D) All of these

3. Find out the OSI layer, which performs token management.
   (A) Network Layer
   (B) Transport Layer
   (C) Session Layer
   (D) Presentation Layer

4. The name of the protocol which provides virtual terminal in TCP/IP model is
   (A) Telnet   (B) SMTP
   (C) HTTP   (D) None of these

5. The layer one of the OSI model is
   (A) Physical layer
   (B) Link layer
   (C) Router layer
   (D) Broadcast layer

6. What is the name of the network topology in which there are bi-directional links between each possible node?
   (A) Ring   (B) Star
   (C) Tree   (D) Mesh

7. What is the commonly used unit for measuring the speed of data transmission?
   (A) Bytes per second
   (B) Baud
   (C) Bits per second
   (D) Both (B) and (C)

8. Which of the communication modes support two way traffic but in only one direction at a time?
   (A) Simplex
   (B) Half-duplex
   (C) Three-quarter's duplex
   (D) Full duplex

9. The loss in signal power as light travels down the fiber is called ________.
   (A) Attenuation   (B) Propagation
   (C) Scattering   (D) Interruption

10. Which of the following TCP/IP protocols is used for transferring files from one machine to another.
   (A) FTP   (B) SNMP
   (C) SMTP   (D) RPC

11. ______ address use 7 bits for the <network> and 24 bits for the <host> portion of the IP address.
   (A) Class A   (B) Class B
   (C) Class C   (D) Class D

12. _____ addresses are reserved for multicasting.
   (A) Class B   (B) Class C
   (C) Class D   (D) Class E

13. Which of the following statements is true?
   (i) An address with all bits 1 is interpreted as all networks or all hosts.
   (ii) The class A network 128.0.0.0 is defined as the loopback network.
   (A) (i) only
   (B) (ii) only
   (C) Both (A) and (B)
   (D) None of these

14. Which is not the Regional Internet Registers (RIR) of the following?
   (A) American Registry for Internet Numbers (ARIN)
   (B) Europeans Registry for Internet Numbers (ERIN)
   (C) Reseaux IP Europeans (RIPE)
   (D) Asia Pacific Network Information Centre (APNIC)

15. Match the following IEEE No to their corresponding Name for IEEE 802 standards for LANs.
   (i)   802.3   (a) WiFi
   (ii) 802.11   (b) WiMa
   (iii) 802.15.1   (c) Ethernet
   (iv) 802.16   (d) Bluetooth
   (A) i–b, ii–c, iii–d, iv–a
   (B) i–c, ii–d, iii–a, iv–b
   (C) i–c, ii–a, iii–d, iv–b
   (D) i–b, ii–d, iii–c, iv–a

16. ______ was the first step in the evolution of Ethernet from a coaxial cable bus to hub managed, twisted pair network.
   (A) Star LAN
   (B) Ring LAN
   (C) Mesh LAN
   (D) All of these

17. ________ is the predominant form of Fast Ethernet, and runs over two pairs of category 5 or above cable.
   (A) 100 BASE–T
   (B) 100 BASE–TX
   (C) 100 BASE–T4
   (D) 100 BASE–T2

18. IEEE 802.3ab defines Gigabit Ethernet transmission over unshielded twisted pair (UTP) category 5, 5e or 6 cabling known as __________.
   (A) 1000 BASE-T
   (B) 1000 BASE-SX
   (C) 1000 BASE-LX
   (D) 1000 BASE-CX

19. Secret-key encryption is also known as
   (A) Asymmetric encryption
   (B) Symmetric encryption
   (C) Secret-encryption
   (D) Private encryption

20. Telnet is a
   (A) Network of Telephones
   (B) Television Network
   (C) Remote Login
   (D) Remote Login

21. A header in CGI script can specify
   (A) Format of the document.
   (B) New location of the document.
   (C) Both (A) and (B)
   (D) Start of the document.

22. In 32 bit IP Addressing scheme, all 1's represent

(A) This computer
(B) Directed broadcast
(C) Limited broadcast
(D) Loop back

23. DMSP stands for
    (A) Distributed Mail System Protocol
    (B) Distributed Message System Protocol
    (C) Distributed Message System Pool
    (D) Distributed Mail System Pool

24. Most segments of a name in DNS represents
    (A) Individual Network
    (B) Individual computer
    (C) Domain name
    (D) Network type

25. Address 192.5.48.3 belongs to
    (A) Class A
    (B) Class B
    (C) Class C
    (D) Class D

26. Which of the following is not a networking device?
    (A) Gateways
    (B) Linux
    (C) Routers
    (D) Firewalls

27. Which of the following is not the External Security Threats?
    (A) Front-door Threats
    (B) Back-door Threats
    (C) Underground Threats
    (D) Denial of Service (DoS)

28. RAID stands for
    (A) Redundant Array of Independent Disks
    (B) Redundant Array of Important Disks
    (C) Random Access of Independent Disks
    (D) Random Access of Important Disks

29. What is the maximum header size of an IP packet?
    (A) 32 bytes
    (B) 64 bytes
    (C) 30 bytes
    (D) 60 bytes

30. What do you mean by broadcasting in networking?
    (A) It means addressing a packet to all machine.
    (B) It means addressing a packet to some machine.
    (C) It means addressing a packet to a particular machine.
    (D) It means addressing a packet to except a particular machine.

HOTS (ACHIEVERS SECTION)

31. State whether the following statements is true or false.
    (i) In class B addresses, a total of more than 1 billion addresses can be formed.
    (ii) Class E addresses are reserved for future or experimental use.
    (A) True, False   (B) True, True
    (C) False, True   (D) False, False

32. What is the demilitarized Zone?
    (A) The area between firewall and connection to an external network
    (B) The area between ISP to Military area
    (C) The area surrounded by secured servers
    (D) The area surrounded by the Military

33. ARP (Address Resolution Protocol) is
    (A) A TCP/IP protocol used to dynamically bind a high level IP address to a low- level physical hardware address
    (B) A TCP/IP high level protocol for transferring files from one machine to another
    (C) A protocol used to monitor computers
    (D) A protocol that handles error and control messages

34. In OSI network architecture, the dialogue control and token management are responsibility of
    (A) Session layer   (B) Network layer
    (C) Transport layer   (D) Data link layer

35. In OSI network architecture, the routing is performed by
    (A) Network layer
    (B) Data link layer
    (C) Transport layer
    (D) Session layer

1.	Ⓐ Ⓑ Ⓒ Ⓓ	8.	Ⓐ Ⓑ Ⓒ Ⓓ	15.	Ⓐ Ⓑ Ⓒ Ⓓ	22	Ⓐ Ⓑ Ⓒ Ⓓ	29.	Ⓐ Ⓑ Ⓒ Ⓓ
2.	Ⓐ Ⓑ Ⓒ Ⓓ	9.	Ⓐ Ⓑ Ⓒ Ⓓ	16.	Ⓐ Ⓑ Ⓒ Ⓓ	23.	Ⓐ Ⓑ Ⓒ Ⓓ	30.	Ⓐ Ⓑ Ⓒ Ⓓ
3.	Ⓐ Ⓑ Ⓒ Ⓓ	10.	Ⓐ Ⓑ Ⓒ Ⓓ	17.	Ⓐ Ⓑ Ⓒ Ⓓ	24.	Ⓐ Ⓑ Ⓒ Ⓓ	31.	Ⓐ Ⓑ Ⓒ Ⓓ
4.	Ⓐ Ⓑ Ⓒ Ⓓ	11.	Ⓐ Ⓑ Ⓒ Ⓓ	18.	Ⓐ Ⓑ Ⓒ Ⓓ	25.	Ⓐ Ⓑ Ⓒ Ⓓ	32.	Ⓐ Ⓑ Ⓒ Ⓓ
5.	Ⓐ Ⓑ Ⓒ Ⓓ	12.	Ⓐ Ⓑ Ⓒ Ⓓ	19.	Ⓐ Ⓑ Ⓒ Ⓓ	26.	Ⓐ Ⓑ Ⓒ Ⓓ	33.	Ⓐ Ⓑ Ⓒ Ⓓ
6.	Ⓐ Ⓑ Ⓒ Ⓓ	13.	Ⓐ Ⓑ Ⓒ Ⓓ	20.	Ⓐ Ⓑ Ⓒ Ⓓ	27.	Ⓐ Ⓑ Ⓒ Ⓓ	34.	Ⓐ Ⓑ Ⓒ Ⓓ
7.	Ⓐ Ⓑ Ⓒ Ⓓ	14.	Ⓐ Ⓑ Ⓒ Ⓓ	21.	Ⓐ Ⓑ Ⓒ Ⓓ	28.	Ⓐ Ⓑ Ⓒ Ⓓ	35.	Ⓐ Ⓑ Ⓒ Ⓓ

PROGRAMMING IN SCRATCH  10

LEARNING OBJECTIVES

- ➤ Basic Concepts of Scratch programming
- ➤ Different Panes and blocks in Scratch
- ➤ Making music with Scratch

MULTIPLE CHOICE QUESTIONS

1. Scratch is a programming language.
   (A) True
   (B) False

2. What is an object in Scratch which performs functions controlled by scripts?

   (A) Scratch   (B) Sprite
   (C) Stage   (D) Script

3. What is the backdrop of a project called?
   (A) Sprite   (B) Script
   (C) Scratch   (D) Stage

4. A collection or stack of blocks that all interlock with one another is called?
   (A) Sprite   (B) Scratch
   (C) Script   (D) Stage

5. A costume is
   (A) a code block
   (B) a different way a sprite looks
   (C) a motion
   (D) a sound

6. Tempo is measured in
   (A) beats per second
   (B) beats per minute
   (C) bytes per second
   (D) bits per second

7. The background of the stage can be changed using the instructions under the _____ block.
   (A) Looks   (B) Pen
   (C) Motion   (D) Events

8. A Scratch script/program begins with _____
   (A) Ask block
   (B) Say block
   (C) Event block
   (D) Control block

9. Scratch 2 project saves the file with file extension _____
   (A) .sb2   (B) .ss2
   (C) .sp2   (D) .sc2

10. Under which block do you find the instructions to change the costume of a Sprite?
    (A) Motion   (B) Looks
    (C) Sound   (D) Events

11. What is the function of the 'when green flag clicked' command block?
    (A) Points sprite in the specified direction
    (B) If condition is true, runs the blocks inside
    (C) Runs the script
    (D) None of the above

12. What is the function of the 'Move 10 steps' command block?
    (A) Runs the blocks inside over and over
    (B) Move spite forward
    (C) Runs script below when specified key is pressed
    (D) None of these

13. What is the function of the 'forever' command block?
    (A) Runs the script inside over and over
    (B) Point sprite in specified direction
    (C) If condition is true, runs the blocks inside
    (D) None of these

14. move 10 steps command can be found under ________ block
    (A) Looks
    (B) Sound
    (C) Pen
    (D) Motion

15. To make the sprite wait for some seconds, you can use wait ___ Seconds. Where can you find the instruction?
    (A) Looks Block
    (B) Control Block
    (C) Motion block
    (D) Events block

HOTS (ACHIEVERS SECTION)

16. Which sprite does the script that is displayed affect?

    (A) Diver 1   (B) Diver 2

17. Look at the Scratch stage below. What is the coordinate of the center of the screen?

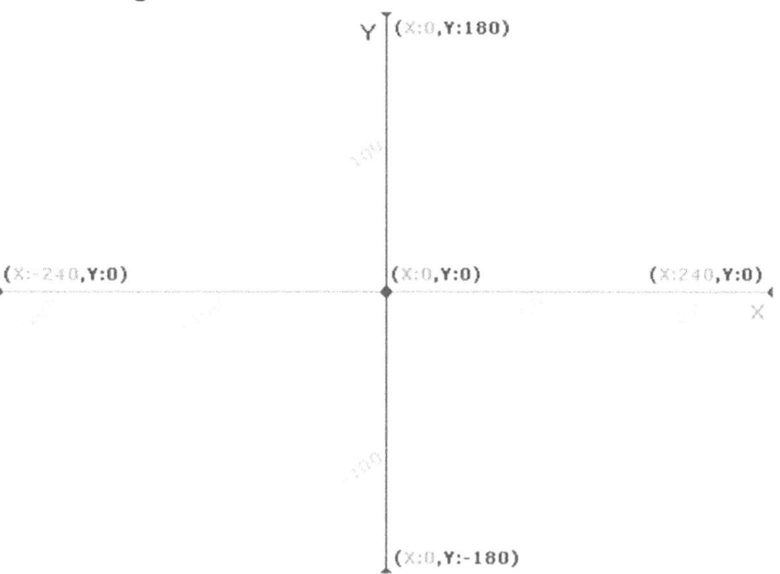

(A) (x:0, Y:–180)   (B) (X:0, Y:0)
(C) (X:240, Y:180)   (D) (X:-240, Y:0)

18. Look at the Scratch stage below. Where on the stage is position (x:240, Y:180)?

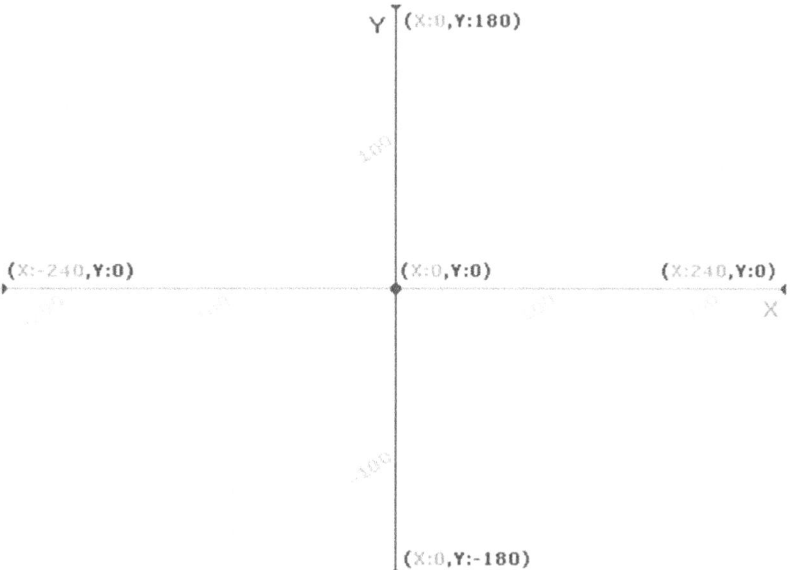

(A) Top Left Corner (B) Bottom Right corner
(C) The top middle   (D) Top Right Corner

19. After the script block has been run, where will the ghost end up?

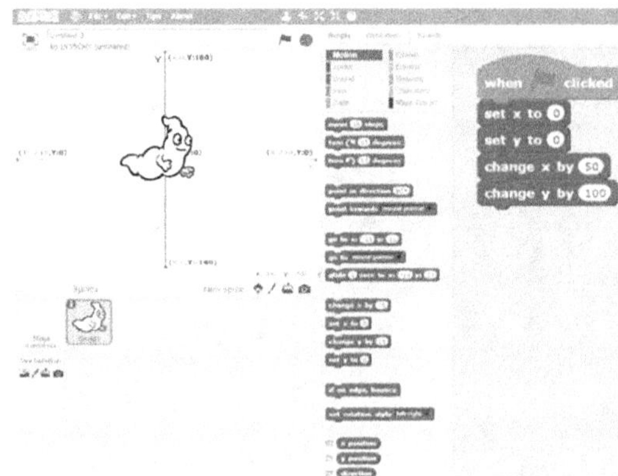

(A) (X:100, Y:50)　　　(B) (X:50, Y:50)
(C) (X:50, Y:100)　　　(D) (X:100, Y:100)

20. The code blocks below are an example of what type of action?

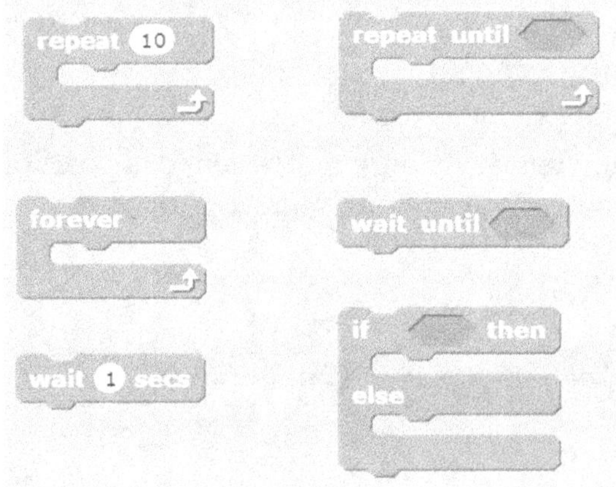

(A) Pen　　　(B) Events
(C) Looks　　　(D) Control

1.	Ⓐ Ⓑ Ⓒ Ⓓ	5.	Ⓐ Ⓑ Ⓒ Ⓓ	9.	Ⓐ Ⓑ Ⓒ Ⓓ	13	Ⓐ Ⓑ Ⓒ Ⓓ	17.	Ⓐ Ⓑ Ⓒ Ⓓ
2.	Ⓐ Ⓑ Ⓒ Ⓓ	6.	Ⓐ Ⓑ Ⓒ Ⓓ	10.	Ⓐ Ⓑ Ⓒ Ⓓ	14.	Ⓐ Ⓑ Ⓒ Ⓓ	18.	Ⓐ Ⓑ Ⓒ Ⓓ
3.	Ⓐ Ⓑ Ⓒ Ⓓ	7.	Ⓐ Ⓑ Ⓒ Ⓓ	11.	Ⓐ Ⓑ Ⓒ Ⓓ	15.	Ⓐ Ⓑ Ⓒ Ⓓ	19.	Ⓐ Ⓑ Ⓒ Ⓓ
4.	Ⓐ Ⓑ Ⓒ Ⓓ	8.	Ⓐ Ⓑ Ⓒ Ⓓ	12.	Ⓐ Ⓑ Ⓒ Ⓓ	16.	Ⓐ Ⓑ Ⓒ Ⓓ	20.	Ⓐ Ⓑ Ⓒ Ⓓ

PROGRAMMING IN PYTHON 

MULTIPLE CHOICE QUESTIONS

1. Who developed Python Programming Language?
   (A) Wick van Rossum
   (B) Rasmus Lerdorf
   (C) Guido van Rossum
   (D) Niene Stom

2. Which type of Programming does Python support?
   (A) Object-oriented programming
   (B) Structured programming
   (C) Functional programming
   (D) All of the mentioned

3. Is Python case sensitive when dealing with identifiers?
   (A) no
   (B) yes
   (C) machine dependent
   (D) none of the mentioned

4. Which of the following is the correct extension of the Python file?
   (A) .python
   (B) .pl
   (C) .py
   (D) .p

5. Is Python code compiled or interpreted?
   (A) Python code is both compiled and interpreted
   (B) Python code is neither compiled nor interpreted
   (C) Python code is only compiled
   (D) Python code is only interpreted

6. All keywords in Python are in __________
   (A) Capitalized
   (B) lower case
   (C) UPPER CASE
   (D) None of the mentioned

7. What will be the value of the following Python expression?
   $4 + 3\% 5$
   (A) 7   (B) 2
   (C) 4   (D) 1

8. Which of the following is used to define a block of code in Python language?
   (A) Indentation
   (B) Key
   (C) Brackets
   (D) All of the mentioned

9. Which keyword is used for function in Python language?

(A) Function   (B) def

(C) Fun   (D) Define

10. Which of the following character is used to give single-line comments in Python?

(A) //   (B) #

(C) !   (D) /*

11. Which of the following functions can help us to find the version of python that we are currently working on?

(A) sys.version(1)

(B) sys.version(0)

(C) sys.version()

(D) sys.version

12. Python supports the creation of anonymous functions at runtime, using a construct called __________

(A) pi

(B) anonymous

(C) lambda

(D) none of the mentioned

13. What is the order of precedence in python?

(A) Exponential, Parentheses, Multiplication, Division, Addition, Subtraction

(B) Exponential, Parentheses, Division, Multiplication, Addition, Subtraction

(C) Parentheses, Exponential, Multiplication, Division, Subtraction, Addition

(D) Parentheses, Exponential, Multiplication, Division, Addition, Subtraction

14. What will be the output of the following Python code snippet if x = 1?

```
x<<2
```

(A) 4   (B) 2

(C) 1   (D) 8

15. What does PIP stand for python?

(A) Pip Installs Python

(B) Pip Installs Packages

(C) Preferred Installer Program

(D) All of the mentioned

16. Which of the following is true for variable names in Python?

(A) Underscore and ampersand are the only two special characters allowed

(B) Unlimited length

(C) All private members must have leading and trailing underscores

(D) None of the mentioned

17. Which of the following is the truncation division operator in Python?

(A) |

(B) //

(C) /

(D) %

18. Which of the following functions is a built-in function in python?

(A) factorial()

(B) print()

(C) seed()

(D) sqrt()

19. Which of the following is the use of id() function in python?

(A) Every object doesn't have a unique id

(B) Id returns the identity of the object

(C) All of the mentioned

(D) None of the mentioned

20. The following python program can work with ______ parameters.

```
def f(x):
def f1(*args, **kwargs):
print("Golu")
return x(*args, **kwargs)
return f1
```

(A) Any number of

(B) 0

(C) 1

(D) 2

21. What will be the output of the following Python function?

    min(max(False,–3,–4), 2,7)

    (A) –4

    (B) –3

    (C) 2

    (D) False

22. Which of the following is not a core data type in Python programming?

    (A) Tuples

    (B) Lists

    (C) Class

    (D) Dictionary

23. What will be the output of the following Python expression if x=56.236?

    print(" %.2f" %x)

    (A) 56.236

    (B) 56.23

    (C) 56.0000

    (D) 56.24

24. Which of these is the definition for packages in Python?

    (A) A set of main modules

    (B) A folder of python modules

    (C) A number of files containing Python definitions and statements

    (D) A set of programs making use of Python modules

25. What will be the output of the following Python function?

    len(["hello",2, 4, 6])

    (A) Error

    (B) 6

    (C) 4

    (D) 3

26. What is the order of namespaces in which Python looks for an identifier?

    (A) Python first searches the built-in namespace, then the global namespace and finally the local namespace

    (B) Python first searches the built-in namespace, then the local namespace and finally the global namespace

    (C) Python first searches the local namespace, then the global namespace and finally the built-in namespace

    (D) Python first searches the global namespace, then the local namespace and finally the built-in namespace

27. What will be the output of the following Python code snippet?

    for i in [1, 2, 3, 4][::-1]:
    print (i)

    (A) 4 3 2 1

    (B) Error

    (C) 1 2 3 4

    (D) none of the mentioned

28. What will be the output of the following Python statement?

    >>>"a"+"bc"

    (A) bc   (B) abc

    (C) a   (D) bca

29. Which function is called when the following Python program is executed?

    f = foo()
    format(f)

    (A) str()   (B) format()

    (C) __str__()   (D) __format__()

30. Which one of the following is not a keyword in Python language?

    (A) pass

    (B) eval

    (C) assert

    (D) nonlocal

31. What will be the output of the following Python program?

```
i = 0
while i < 5:
print(i)
i += 1
if i == 3:
break
else:
print(0)
```

(A) Error

(B) 0 1 2 0

(C) 0 1 2

(D) none of the mentioned

32. Which of the following Python statements will result in the output: 6?

```
A = [[1, 2, 3], [4, 5, 6], [7, 8, 9]]
```

(A) A[2][1]   (B) A[1][2]

(C) A[3][2]   (D) A[2][3]

33. What will be the output of the following Python code?

```
>>>list1 = [1, 3]
>>>list2 = list1
>>>list1[0] = 4
>>>print(list2)
```

(A) [1, 4]   (B) [1, 3, 4]

(C) [4, 3]   (D) [1, 3]

34. What will be the output of the following Python code?

```
l=[1, 0, 2, 0, 'hello', '', []]
list(filter(bool, l))
```

(A) [1, 0, 2, 'hello', '', []]

(B) Error

(C) [1, 2, 'hello']

(D) [1, 0, 2, 0, 'hello', '', []]

35. What will be the output of the following Python code?

```
i = 1
while True:
if i%3 == 0:
break
print(i)
i + = 1
```

(A) 1 2 3

(B) Error

(C) 1 2

(D) None of the mentioned

1.	(A) (B) (C) (D)	8.	(A) (B) (C) (D)	15.	(A) (B) (C) (D)	22	(A) (B) (C) (D)	29.	(A) (B) (C) (D)
2.	(A) (B) (C) (D)	9.	(A) (B) (C) (D)	16.	(A) (B) (C) (D)	23.	(A) (B) (C) (D)	30.	(A) (B) (C) (D)
3.	(A) (B) (C) (D)	10.	(A) (B) (C) (D)	17.	(A) (B) (C) (D)	24.	(A) (B) (C) (D)	31.	(A) (B) (C) (D)
4.	(A) (B) (C) (D)	11.	(A) (B) (C) (D)	18.	(A) (B) (C) (D)	25.	(A) (B) (C) (D)	32.	(A) (B) (C) (D)
5.	(A) (B) (C) (D)	12.	(A) (B) (C) (D)	19.	(A) (B) (C) (D)	26.	(A) (B) (C) (D)	33.	(A) (B) (C) (D)
6.	(A) (B) (C) (D)	13.	(A) (B) (C) (D)	20.	(A) (B) (C) (D)	27.	(A) (B) (C) (D)	34.	(A) (B) (C) (D)
7.	(A) (B) (C) (D)	14.	(A) (B) (C) (D)	21.	(A) (B) (C) (D)	28.	(A) (B) (C) (D)	35.	(A) (B) (C) (D)

LATEST DEVELOPMENTS IN THE FIELD OF 'IT'

LEARNING OBJECTIVES

➤ Latest developments in the field of IT

MULTIPLE CHOICE QUESTIONS

1. What was Google Day-Dream?

   (A) It is an instant messaging app launched by Google.

   (B) It is a virtual reality platform.

   (C) It is an intelligent personal assistant.

   (D) It is a mobile app that presents view of galaxy at both day and night time.

2. __________ sensor available in smartphones detects the presence of nearby objects without any physical contacts.

   (A) Proximity

   (B) Reflexive

   (C) Predictive

   (D) Magnetometer

3. Which of the following statements holds true about the given logo?

   ![SanDisk logo]

   Statement 1: It is a freeware web browser for Windows and OS X platforms.

   Statement 2: It is also available on Windows Phone 8, iOS and Android platforms as Maxthon Mobile.

   (A) Only Statement 1

   (B) Only Statement 2

   (C) Both Statement 1 and Statement 2

   (D) Neither Statement 1 nor Statement 2

4. Which of the following features is available in Windows 8.1?

   (A) Miracast Streaming

   (B) Wi-Fi Direct

   (C) 3D printing

   (D) All of these

5. Gaining website traffic or attention through media sites is generally referred to as __________.

   (A) Search analytics

   (B) Web analytics

   (C) Social media marketing

   (D) Contextual advertising

6. Which of the following programs is used to produce automated posts on the Twitter microblogging service and to automatically follow Twitter users?

   (A) Botnet

   (B) Twitterbot

   (C) Twitgear

   (D) Twitteroid

7. Which of the following is a hosted online version of the Microsoft Office with access to Word, Excel, PowerPoint, etc.?
   (A) Office 460   (B) Office 365
   (C) Office 565   (D) Office 2015

8. _________refers to an electronic environment that are sensitive and responsive to the presence of people.
   (A) Ambient Intelligent
   (B) Fog Computing
   (C) Semantic Web
   (D) Nano Computing

9. _________ is a navigation system used to locate objects or people inside a building using radio waves or sensory information collected by mobile devices.
   (A) Indoor Positioning System
   (B) Intelligent Access System
   (C) Mobile Planetary System
   (D) Space Position System

10. Which of the following is a proprietary computer software package for remote control, desktop sharing, online meetings, web conferencing and file transfer between computers?
   (A) Cisco   (B) Moodle
   (C) TeamViewer   (D) WiZiQ

11. _________ is a network security measure, employed on one or more computers to ensure that a secure computer network is physically isolated from unsecured networks, such as unsecured LAN.
   (A) Air side   (B) Secure site
   (C) Air gap   (D) Air process

12. A "Motion sensing" input device for Xbox 360 and Xbox One which enables users to control and interact with their console without the need of game controller.
   (A) Binect   (B) Kinect
   (C) Dinect   (D) Connect

13. Which of the following is the primary controller of PlayStation 4, the latest video game console by Sony?
   (A) Shockwave
   (B) Dual 4
   (C) Dual Shock 4
   (D) Playwave

14. Which of the following Google's product allowed you to set time or location-based reminders for notes?
   (A) Google Blips
   (B) Google Glass
   (C) Google Play
   (D) Google Keep

15. _________is the latest release of Bluetooth Technology standard as of June 2016.
   (A) 4.1   (B) 4.2
   (C) 5   (D) 6

16. _________is a thumb-sized media streaming device by Google.
   (A) Caster   (B) ChromeCast
   (C) GoogleDigi   (D) GoCast

17. What is Bharat Net?
   (A) Used for the growth of the Indian IT companies
   (B) Used for development of technologies
   (C) Used for connecting the employees globally
   (D) Used for connecting the rural area through broad band

18. What is the tool used for Multi-Platform Mobile App Development?
   (A) Sketch   (B) Configure. IT
   (C) Django   (D) Invision

19. What is SNOW-FOX?
   (A) Mobile phone
   (B) Operating system
   (C) Android app
   (D) Android name

20. Which of the following can be used to speed the running of an app?
   (A) Docker
   (B) Genwi
   (C) Xcode
   (D) Gene motion

21. How can you assemble the mock-ups on your phone?
    (A) Acorn4 (B) Fluid UI
    (C) Wearable's (D) Block chain

22. What technology is used to modify the images and the PNG files in Android?
    (A) Genwi (B) Django
    (C) Acorn4 (D) Fluid UI

23. While developing an app, if you have undergone a crash, then which of the following option will you use to report the problem?

    (A) Appcelerator (B) Unity
    (C) Ubertesters (D) Crashlytics

24. What is the best tool to develop Android games in C++ using Android devices?
    (A) Qt.Framework (B) Gamesalad
    (C) Adobe-Air (D) Configure-IT

25. Which of the tools can support a desktop version?
    (A) Cocos2D (B) Remix-OS
    (C) Configure. IT (D) Acorn4

Darken Your Choice with HB Pencil

1. Ⓐ Ⓑ Ⓒ Ⓓ	6. Ⓐ Ⓑ Ⓒ Ⓓ	11. Ⓐ Ⓑ Ⓒ Ⓓ	16 Ⓐ Ⓑ Ⓒ Ⓓ	21. Ⓐ Ⓑ Ⓒ Ⓓ
2. Ⓐ Ⓑ Ⓒ Ⓓ	7. Ⓐ Ⓑ Ⓒ Ⓓ	12. Ⓐ Ⓑ Ⓒ Ⓓ	17. Ⓐ Ⓑ Ⓒ Ⓓ	22. Ⓐ Ⓑ Ⓒ Ⓓ
3. Ⓐ Ⓑ Ⓒ Ⓓ	8. Ⓐ Ⓑ Ⓒ Ⓓ	13. Ⓐ Ⓑ Ⓒ Ⓓ	18. Ⓐ Ⓑ Ⓒ Ⓓ	23. Ⓐ Ⓑ Ⓒ Ⓓ
4. Ⓐ Ⓑ Ⓒ Ⓓ	9. Ⓐ Ⓑ Ⓒ Ⓓ	14. Ⓐ Ⓑ Ⓒ Ⓓ	19. Ⓐ Ⓑ Ⓒ Ⓓ	24. Ⓐ Ⓑ Ⓒ Ⓓ
5. Ⓐ Ⓑ Ⓒ Ⓓ	10. Ⓐ Ⓑ Ⓒ Ⓓ	15. Ⓐ Ⓑ Ⓒ Ⓓ	20. Ⓐ Ⓑ Ⓒ Ⓓ	25. Ⓐ Ⓑ Ⓒ Ⓓ

LOGICAL REASONING

LEARNING OBJECTIVES

- Different types of Relationships
- Letter Analogy
- Word Analogy
- Classification concept and its examples
- Pattern series
- Alphabet series
- Tips to solve Coding and Decoding
- Alphabet Type questions
- Number ranking
- Different types of blood relation
- Different directions and their examples
- Different types of Figure pattern questions
- Cube type questions and their types
- Dice based questions
- Mirror images of letters and numbers
- Water images of letters and numbers

MULTIPLE CHOICE QUESTIONS

Direction (1–5): In the following questions, choose the word that shows the same relationship as given in the each question.

1. **Bank** is related to **Money** in the same way as **Transport** is related to
   (A) Goods   (B) Road
   (C) Terrace   (D) Floor

2. **Euro** is related to **Italy** in the same way as **Taka** is related to
   (A) Pakistan   (B) Jordan
   (C) Mexico   (D) Bangladesh

3. **Needle** is related to **Clock** as **Wheel** is related to ______
   (A) Drive   (B) Vehicle
   (C) Circular   (D) Move

4. **Disease** is related to **pathology** in the same way as **Planet** is related to
   (A) Sun   (B) Satellite
   (C) Astrology   (D) Astronomy

5. **Boat** is related to **Oar** in the same way as **Bicycle** is related to
   (A) Road   (B) Wheel
   (C) Seat   (D) Pedal

Direction (6-10): Three out of the four alternatives are same in a certain way and so form a group. Find the odd one that does not belong to the group.

6. (A) Gold   (B) Silver
   (C) Bronze   (D) Iron

7. (A) Yen   (B) Lira
   (C) Dollar   (D) Ounce

8. (A) Huge   (B) Tiny
   (C) Heavy   (D) Small

OLYMPIAD WORKBOOK (NCO) CLASS – 10

9.   (A) Teeth   (B) Tongue
    (C) Palate   (D) Chin

10. (A) Silk   (B) Cotton
    (C) Nylon   (D) Wool

Direction (11-15): Find the missing numbers From the given alternatives

11. 2, 8, 18, 32, ?
    (A) 62   (B) 60
    (C) 50   (D) 46

12. 16, 54, 195, ?
    (A) 780   (B) 802
    (C) 816   (D) 824

13. 14, 316, 536, 764, ?
    (A) 981   (B) 1048
    (C) 8110   (D) 9100

14. 8, 11, 15, 22, 33, 51, ?, 127, 203
    (A) 80   (B) 53
    (C) 58   (D) 69

15. 2, 3, 6, 18, ?, 1944
    (A) 154   (B) 180
    (C) 108   (D) 452

16. If in any code language, TARGET is coded as UYUCJN, then how will VICTORY be written in that code?
    (A) UKZXJXR
    (B) UKYXJDR
    (C) UKYXJWD
    (D) None

17. If in a certain code MANISH is written as NZMRHS, then how will RANJITA be written in that code?
    (A) IZMQRGZ
    (B) IZMPRGZ
    (C) IZMQRHZ
    (D) IZMQRIZ

18. If MENTAL is written LNDFMOSUZBKM, then how will TEST be written in that code?

(A) UVFGTIIV
(B) RSCDQRRS
(B) SUDFRQRSM
(D) SUDFRTSU

19. If HERCULES is coded s JCTAWJGQ, then how will APHRODITE be written in that code?
    (A) CNMJTBKRG
    (B) CNJMTBKSG
    (C) CNJMTBKRG
    (D) CNJMTCKRG

20. If BOX is coded as CDPQYZ, what will be the last two letters of word in the same code for HERO?
    (A) N, M   (B) M, N
    (C) P, Q   (D) Q, P

21. Arrange the given words in alphabetical order and tick the one that comes last.
    (A) Plane   (B) Plain
    (C) Player   (D) Place

Direction (22–23): In following two questions, a group of letters is given, which are numbered 1, 2, 3, 4, 5 and 6. Below are given four alternatives containing combinations of these numbers. Select the combination of numbers so that letters arranged accordingly form a meaningful word.

22. G A N I M E
    1 2 3 4 5 6
    (A) 1, 2, 4, 3, 6, 5
    (B) 6, 3, 4, 1, 5, 2
    (C) 5, 2, 1, 4, 3, 6
    (D) 2, 5, 1, 4, 3, 6

23. C E L S M U
    1 2 3 4 5 6
    (A) 4, 6, 3, 5, 2, 1
    (B) 5, 6, 4, 1, 3, 2
    (C) 4, 6, 5, 2, 3, 1
    (D) 5, 2, 3, 1, 6, 4

24. How many pairs of letter are there in the word, 'EXPERIENCED' which have as many letters between them in the word as in the alphabet?

(A) One

(B) Three

(C) Four

(D) More than four

25. How many pairs of letters are there in the word REPURCUSSION which have as many letters between them in the word as in the alphabet?

(A) Three

(B) One

(C) Two

(D) More than three

26. Akash said to Mohit, "That boy in blue shirt is younger of the two brothers of the daughter of my father's wife". How is the boy in blue shirt related to Aakash?

(A) Father　　　　(B) Uncle

(C) Brother　　　　(D) Nephew

27. Pointing to a person, Rohit said to Neha' "His mother is the only daughter of your father, How is Neha related to that person?

(A) Aunt　　　　(B) Mother

(C) Daughter　　　　(D) Wife

28. 'P + Q' means 'P is the brother of Q'. 'P − Q means P is the mother of Q and 'P × Q' means 'P is the sister of Q'. Which of the following means that M is the maternal uncle of R?

(A) M − R + K

(B) M + K − R

(C) M + K × Q

(D) None of these

29. 'A + B' means 'A is the son of B', 'A − B' means 'A is the wife of B'. 'A × B' means 'A is the brother of B', 'A ÷ B' means 'A is the mother of B', 'A = B' means 'A is the sister of B'. Which of the following represents P as the maternal uncle of Q?

(A) R × P ÷ Q

(B) P × R ÷ Q

(C) P + R ÷ Q

(D) P + R × Q

30. Amit said, "This girl is the wife of the grandson of my mother." How is Amit related to the girl?

(A) Father

(B) Father-in-law

(C) Grandfather

(D) Husband

31. One evening before sunset, two friends Amit and Sunit were talking to each other face to face. If Sunil's shadow was exactly to his left side, which direction was Amit facing?

(A) North

(B) South

(C) West

(D) Data inadequate

32. A postman was returning to the post office which was in front of him to the North. When the post office was 100 m away from him, he turned to the left and moved 50 m to deliver the last letter at Shantivilla. He then moved in the same direction for 40 m, turned to his right and moved 100 m. How many m was he away from the post office?

(A) 0　　　　　　　(B) 90

(C) 150　　　　　　(D) 100

33. Two buses start from the opposite points of a main road, 150 km apart. The first bus runs for 25 km and takes a turn right and runs for 15 km. It then turns left and runs for another 25 km and takes the direction back to reach the main

road. In the meantime, due to a minor breakdown, the other bus has run only 35 km along the main road, what would be the distance between the two buses at this point?

(A) 75 km (B) 80 km
(C) 65 km (D) 85 km

34. A man is facing West. He turns 450 m in the clockwise direction and then another 1800 m in the same direction and then 2700 m in the anticlockwise direction. Which direction is he facing now?

(A) South (B) North-West
(C) West (D) South-West

35. A started from a place. After walking for a kilometer, he turned to the left, then walked for a half km. He again turned to the left. Now, he went to the Eastward direction. In which direction, did he originally start?

(A) West (B) East
(C) South (D) North

36. Find the day of the week on 26 January, 1995.

(A) Tuesday (B) Friday
(C) Wednesday (D) Thursday

37. Which two months in a year have the same calendar?

(A) June, October
(B) April, November
(C) April, July
(D) October, December

38. Are the years 900 and 1000 leap years?

(A) Yes (B) No
(C) Can't say (D) None of these

39. If it was Saturday on 17th November, 1962, what will be the day on 22nd November, 1964?

(A) Monday (B) Tuesday
(C) Wednesday (D) Sunday

40. Sangeeta remembers that her father's birthday was certainly after eight but before thirteenth of December. Her sister Natasha remembers that their father's birthday was definitely after ninth but before fourteenth of December. On which date of December was their father's birthday?

(A) 10th
(B) 11th
(C) 12th
(D) Data inadequate

Direction (41-45): Each of the following questions consists of five figures marked 1, 2, 3, 4 and 5. These figures form a series. Find out the one from the answer figures that will continue the series.

41. Problem Figures:

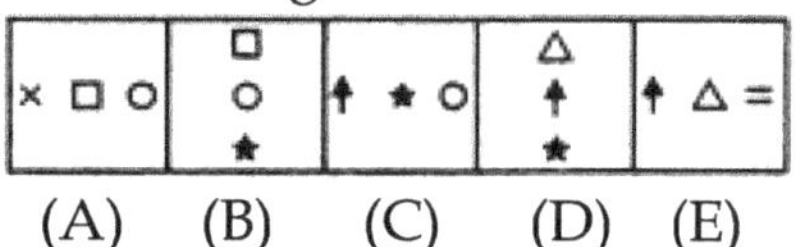

(A) (B) (C) (D) (E)

Answer Figures:

(1) (2) (3) (4) (5)

(A) 1 (B) 2
(C) 3 (D) 4
(E) 5

42. Problem Figures:

(A) (B) (C) (D) (E)

Answer Figures:

(1) (2) (3) (4) (5)

(A) 1 (B) 2
(C) 3 (D) 4
(E) 5

43. Problem Figures:

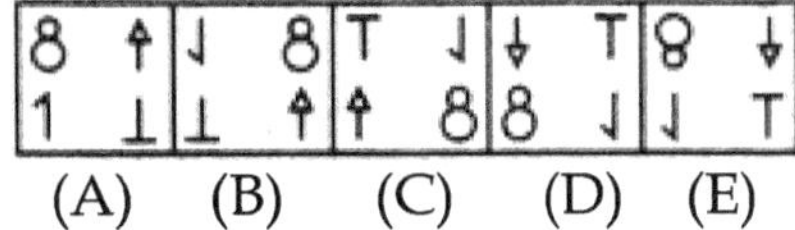

   (A)   (B)   (C)   (D)   (E)

Answer Figures:

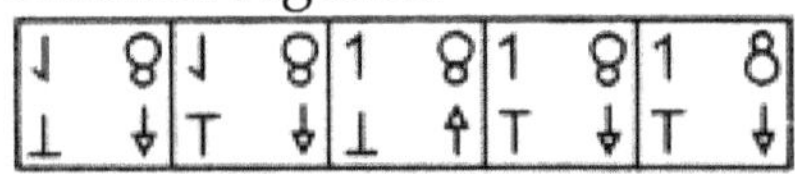

   (1)   (2)   (3)   (4)   (5)

(A) 1   (B) 2
(C) 3   (D) 4
(E) 5

44. Problem Figures:

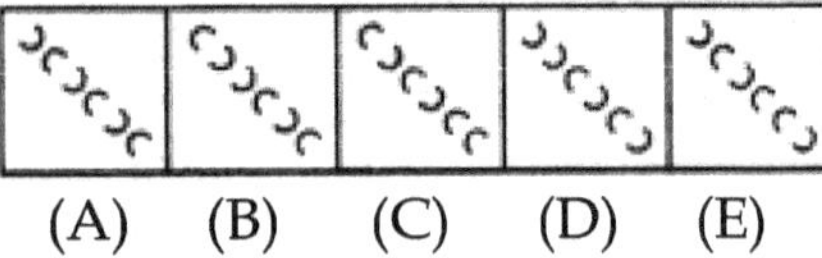

   (A)   (B)   (C)   (D)   (E)

Answer Figures:

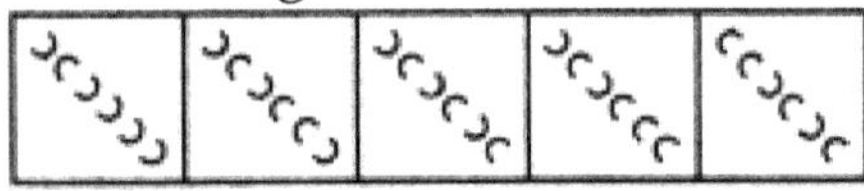

   (1)   (2)   (3)   (4)   (5)

(A) 1   (B) 2
(C) 3   (D) 4
(E) 5

45. Problem Figures:

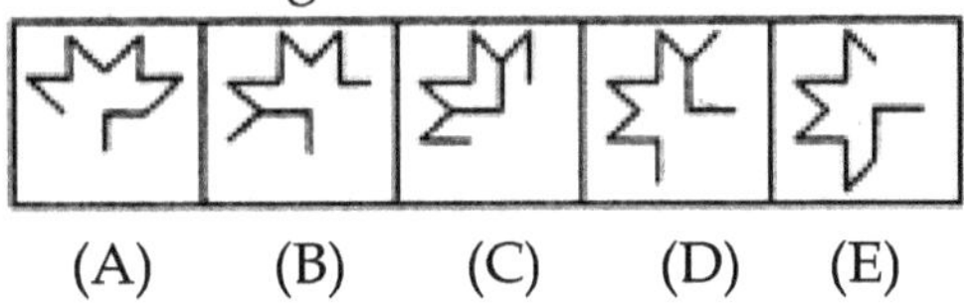

   (A)   (B)   (C)   (D)   (E)

46. How many squares are there in the following figure?

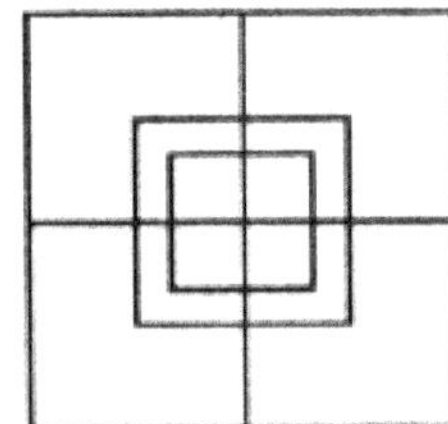

(A) 13   (B) 14
(C) 16   (D) 15

47. Count the number of triangles and squares in the following figure.

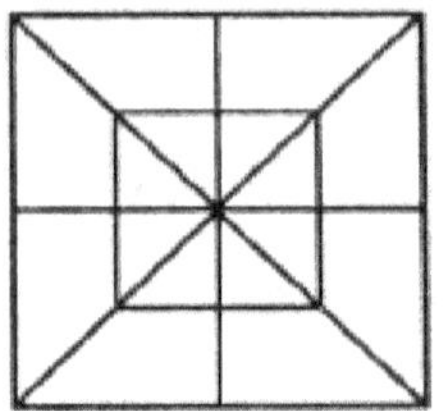

(A) 28 triangles, 10 squares
(B) 28 triangles, 8 squares
(C) 32 triangles, 10 squares
(D) 32 triangles, 8 squares

48. Count the number of squares in the following figure.

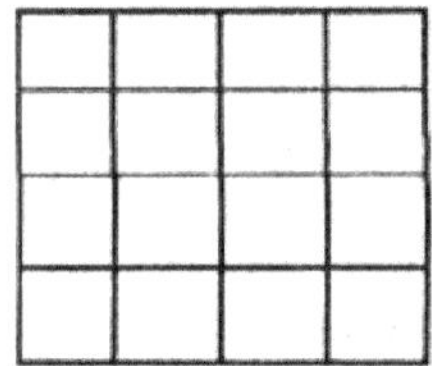

(A) 16   (B) 17
(C) 30   (D) 55

49. Count the number of straight lines and triangles in the following figure.

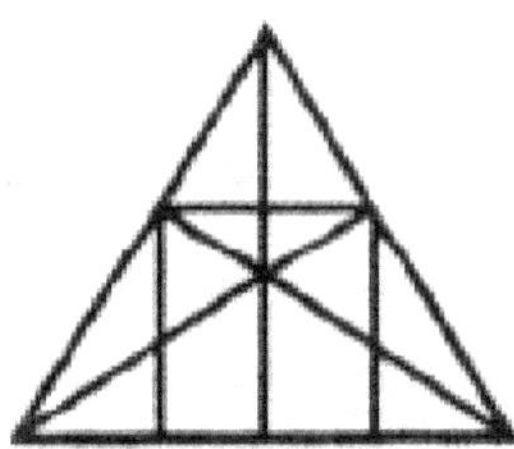

(A) 10 straight lines and 34 triangles
(B) 9 straight lines and 34 triangles
(C) 9 straight lines and 36 triangles
(D) 10 straight lines and 36 triangles

50. How many triangles and squares are there in the following figure?

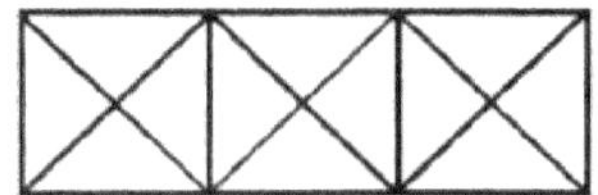

(A) 28 triangles, 5 squares
(B) 24 triangles, 4 squares
(C) 28 triangles, 4 squares
(D) 24 triangles, 5 squares

Direction (51–55): A cube is coloured orange on one face, pink on the opposite face, brown on one face and silver on a face adjacent to the brown face. The other two faces are left uncoloured. It is then cut into 125 smaller cubes of equal size. Now answer the following questions based on the above statements.

51. How many cubes have at least one face coloured pink?
    (A) 1   (B) 9
    (C) 16   (D) 25

52. How many cubes have all the faces uncoloured?
    (A) 24   (B) 36
    (C) 48   (D) 64

53. How many cubes have at least two faces coloured?
    (A) 19   (B) 20
    (C) 21   (D) 23

54. How many cubes are coloured orange on one face and have the remaining faces uncoloured?
    (A) 8   (B) 12
    (C) 14   (D) 16

55. How many cubes are coloured silver on one face, orange or pink on another face and have four uncoloured faces?
    (A) 8   (B) 10
    (C) 12   (D) 16

Direction (56–60): Choose the correct mirror image from alternatives a, b, c, and d of the given words and figures.

56. VINAYAKA
    (A) INVAYAKA   (B) AKAYANIV
    (C) AKAYANIV   (D) AKAYANIV

57. VERBAL
    (A) LABREV   (B) LRVEBA
    (C) REVBAL   (D) VERBAL

58. CONSOLIDATE
    (A) ETADILOSNOC
    (B) CONSOLIDATE
    (C) TAECONSOLID
    (D) OCNSOLIDATE

59. JUDGEMENT
    (A) TNEMEGDUJ   (B) TJUDGEMEN
    (C) JUDGEMENT   (D) DJUGEMNET

60. TARAIN1014A
    (A) AN4101IARAT   (B) A4101NIARAT
    (C) A410ARTAIN1   (D) A4101NIARAT

—Darken Your Choice with HB Pencil—

1. Ⓐ Ⓑ Ⓒ Ⓓ	13. Ⓐ Ⓑ Ⓒ Ⓓ	25. Ⓐ Ⓑ Ⓒ Ⓓ	37. Ⓐ Ⓑ Ⓒ Ⓓ	49. Ⓐ Ⓑ Ⓒ Ⓓ
2. Ⓐ Ⓑ Ⓒ Ⓓ	14. Ⓐ Ⓑ Ⓒ Ⓓ	26. Ⓐ Ⓑ Ⓒ Ⓓ	38. Ⓐ Ⓑ Ⓒ Ⓓ	50. Ⓐ Ⓑ Ⓒ Ⓓ
3. Ⓐ Ⓑ Ⓒ Ⓓ	15. Ⓐ Ⓑ Ⓒ Ⓓ	27. Ⓐ Ⓑ Ⓒ Ⓓ	39. Ⓐ Ⓑ Ⓒ Ⓓ	51. Ⓐ Ⓑ Ⓒ Ⓓ
4. Ⓐ Ⓑ Ⓒ Ⓓ	16. Ⓐ Ⓑ Ⓒ Ⓓ	28. Ⓐ Ⓑ Ⓒ Ⓓ	40. Ⓐ Ⓑ Ⓒ Ⓓ	52. Ⓐ Ⓑ Ⓒ Ⓓ
5. Ⓐ Ⓑ Ⓒ Ⓓ	17. Ⓐ Ⓑ Ⓒ Ⓓ	29. Ⓐ Ⓑ Ⓒ Ⓓ	41. Ⓐ Ⓑ Ⓒ Ⓓ	53. Ⓐ Ⓑ Ⓒ Ⓓ
6. Ⓐ Ⓑ Ⓒ Ⓓ	18. Ⓐ Ⓑ Ⓒ Ⓓ	30. Ⓐ Ⓑ Ⓒ Ⓓ	42. Ⓐ Ⓑ Ⓒ Ⓓ	54. Ⓐ Ⓑ Ⓒ Ⓓ
7. Ⓐ Ⓑ Ⓒ Ⓓ	19. Ⓐ Ⓑ Ⓒ Ⓓ	31. Ⓐ Ⓑ Ⓒ Ⓓ	43. Ⓐ Ⓑ Ⓒ Ⓓ	55. Ⓐ Ⓑ Ⓒ Ⓓ
8. Ⓐ Ⓑ Ⓒ Ⓓ	20. Ⓐ Ⓑ Ⓒ Ⓓ	32. Ⓐ Ⓑ Ⓒ Ⓓ	44. Ⓐ Ⓑ Ⓒ Ⓓ	56. Ⓐ Ⓑ Ⓒ Ⓓ
9. Ⓐ Ⓑ Ⓒ Ⓓ	21. Ⓐ Ⓑ Ⓒ Ⓓ	33. Ⓐ Ⓑ Ⓒ Ⓓ	45. Ⓐ Ⓑ Ⓒ Ⓓ	57. Ⓐ Ⓑ Ⓒ Ⓓ
10. Ⓐ Ⓑ Ⓒ Ⓓ	22. Ⓐ Ⓑ Ⓒ Ⓓ	34. Ⓐ Ⓑ Ⓒ Ⓓ	46 Ⓐ Ⓑ Ⓒ Ⓓ	58. Ⓐ Ⓑ Ⓒ Ⓓ
11. Ⓐ Ⓑ Ⓒ Ⓓ	23. Ⓐ Ⓑ Ⓒ Ⓓ	35. Ⓐ Ⓑ Ⓒ Ⓓ	47. Ⓐ Ⓑ Ⓒ Ⓓ	59. Ⓐ Ⓑ Ⓒ Ⓓ
12. Ⓐ Ⓑ Ⓒ Ⓓ	24. Ⓐ Ⓑ Ⓒ Ⓓ	36. Ⓐ Ⓑ Ⓒ Ⓓ	48 Ⓐ Ⓑ Ⓒ Ⓓ	60. Ⓐ Ⓑ Ⓒ Ⓓ

MULTIPLE CHOICE QUESTIONS

1. An intelligence agency forms a code of two distinct digits selected from 0, 1, 2, ..., 9 such that the first digit of the code is non-zero. The code, handwritten on a slip, can however potentially create confusion when read upside down – for example, the code 91 may appears as 16. How many codes are there for which no such confusion can arise?
   (A) 80
   (B) 78
   (C) 71
   (D) 69

2. The polynomial $f(x)$ has roots of equations 3, –3, –k. Given that the coefficient of x^3 is 2, and that f(x) has a remainder of 8 when divided by $x + 1$, find the value of k.
   (A) 1
   (B) 0
   (C) –1
   (D) Can't be determined

3. If one of the roots of the equation $3x^3 + 11x^2 + 12x + 4 = 0$ is –1, then the other two roots are __________.
   (A) –2, 2/3
   (B) 2, –2/3
   (C) 2, 2/3
   (D) –2, –2/3

4. A dice is thrown two times. What is the probability of getting sum less than to a fifth multiple of 2?
   (A) 5/6
   (B) 1/6
   (C) 2/3
   (D) 1/3

5. With the vertices of a $\triangle ABC$ as centres, three circles are described, each touching the other two externally. If the sides of the triangle are 4, 6 and 8 cm respectively, then the sum of the radii of the three circles equals __________.
   (A) 10
   (B) 14
   (C) 12
   (D) 9

6. If the straight lines $y = 4 - 3x$; $ay = x + 10$; $2y + bx + 9 = 0$ represent the three consecutive sides of a rectangle & if a is half of b, then $ab = $ _____.
   (A) 18
   (B) –3
   (C) 1/2
   (D) –1/3

7. In given figure, S and T trisect the side QR of a right triangle PQR, then $3PR^2 + 5PS^2 = $

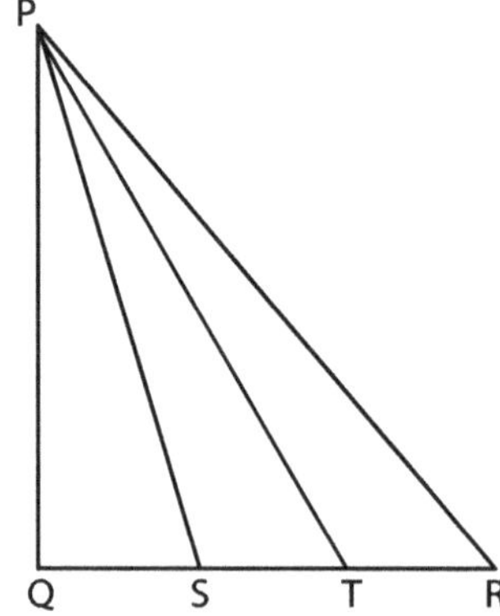

   (A) $4PT^2$
   (B) $8PT^2$
   (C) $8PT$
   (D) None of these

8. Two dice are thrown simultaneously. Find the probability of getting two prime numbers on both dice.
   (A) 5/2
   (B) 1/2
   (C) 5/12
   (D) 1/4

9. The cubic polynomial $f(x)$ is such that $(x + 1)$, $(x - 2)$, $(x + k)$ are factors of $f(x)$ and the coefficient of x^3 is -2. Given that $f(x)$ has a remainder of 20 when divided by $x - 4$, then the value of k is ______.
   (A) 2   (B) -5
   (C) 5   (D) -1

10. An object is observed from three points A, B, C in the same horizontal line passing through the base of the object. The angle of elevation at B is twice and at C thrice that at A. If AB = a, BC = b prove that the height of the object is ________.
    (A) $2a \sin\theta \cos\theta$
    (B) $2a \sin\theta$
    (C) $2a \cos\theta$
    (D) None of these

11. There is a series which begins with unmarked figure on the extreme left. One and only one of the four marked figures does not fit into the series. The two unmarked figures, one each on the extreme left and extreme right fit into the series. You have to take as many aspects into account as possible of the figures in the series and find out the one and only one of the four marked figures which does not fit into the series.

Problem Figures

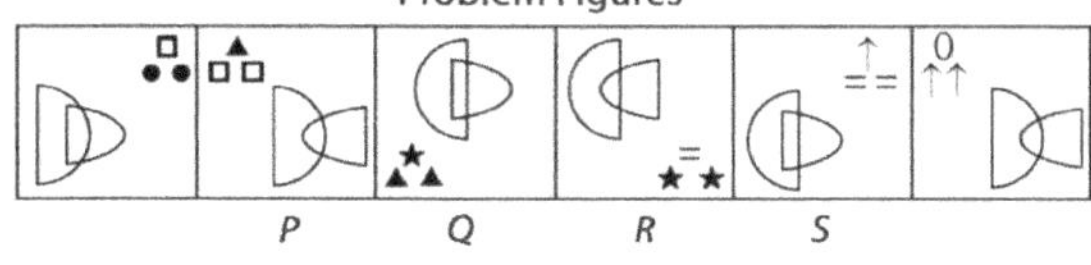

   (A) P   (B) Q
   (C) R   (D) S

12. Kirti is taller than Kanika who is shorter than Kajal. Komal is taller than Kanchan but shorter than Kanika. Who among the following is the shortest?
    (A) Kirti   (B) Kajal
    (C) Kanchan   (D) Kanika

13. Nimish wants to go to school from his house. First of all he goes to the crossing; from here he turns to right and reaches the bus-stand. Bus-stand is opposite to the library. In which direction is school located?
    (A) North
    (B) East
    (C) West
    (D) Cannot be determined

14. The number of squares and triangles in the following figure are ______.

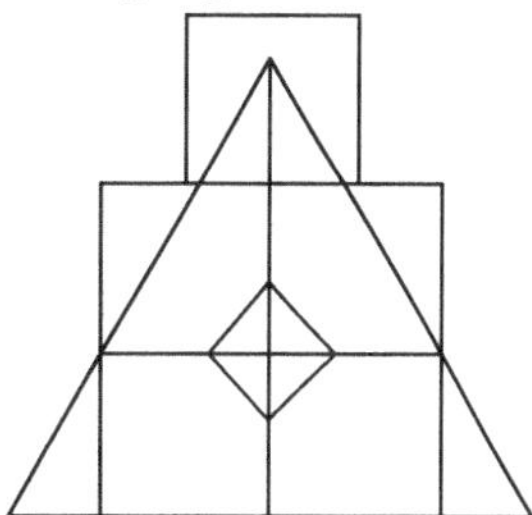

    (A) 7 squares, 18 triangles
    (B) 7 squares, 19 triangles
    (C) 8 squares, 17 triangles
    (D) None of these

15. In the following question, one set of letters, when sequentially placed at the gaps in the given letter series, shall complete it. Identify that set.
    ab _ ab _ ab abb _ b _ ab
    (A) baaa   (B) abbb
    (C) aaab   (D) baab

16. In the following number series, one number does not follow the pattern of the series. Find the wrong number.
    297, 272, 245, 216, 185, 153, 117
    (A) 117   (B) 153
    (C) 185   (D) 216

17. Ravi's brother is 3 years senior to him. His father was 28 years of age when his sister born, while his mother was 26 years of age when he born. If his sister was 4 years of age when his brother was born, what was the age of Ravi's father and mother respectively when his brother was born?
    (A) 32 years, 29 years
    (B) 32 years, 30 years
    (C) 32 years, 23 years
    (D) 35 years, 33 years

18. By following certain logic, 'Take Bath And Do worship of The Goddess' is decoded as 'And Bath Do Goddess of Take The worship.' How will 'Then Why Did You Not Do Your Study' be decoded using that logic?
    (A) Did Do Not Then Study Why You Your
    (B) Do Did Not Study Then You Your Why
    (C) Did Do Not Study Then Why You Your
    (D) Do Did Not Study Then Your You Why

19. A bird shooter was asked number of birds he had in the bag. He replied that there were all sparrows but six, all pigeons but six, and all ducks but six. How many birds he had in all?
    (A) 9
    (B) 18
    (C) 27
    (D) None of these

20. In the following number series how many such 7's are there which are preceded by an odd number and followed by an even number?
    2 4 5 3 7 6 3 2 5 7 3 5 4 2 3 4 5 3 6 7 3 5 7 3 9 3
    (A) 2   (B) 3
    (C) 1   (D) 4

21. ______________ are programs that automatically scan websites and create indexes of URLs, keywords and links.
    (A) Crawlers
    (B) MetaTags
    (C) Browsers
    (D) Search Engines

22. What pages would be listed when you enter the following search term in www.google.co.in?
    President AND (Patil OR Kalam)
    (A) It will list all pages containing 'President Patil' and 'President Kalam'.
    (B) It will list all pages containing 'President Patil Kalam'.
    (C) It will list all pages containing 'President Patil' and not 'President Kalam'.
    (D) It will list all pages containing 'President Patil' or 'President Kalam'.

23. Choose the correct HTML syntax to left-align the content inside a table cell.
    (A) <td valign="left">
    (B) <td align="left">
    (C) <td leftalign>
    (D) <tdleft>

24. In the given example of a section of MS-Excel worksheet how do you change the column width to fit the contents?
    (A) Double-click the boundary to the right of the column heading.
    (B) Press ALT and single-click anywhere in the column.
    (C) Single-click the boundary to the left of the column heading.
    (D) Double-click the boundary to the left of the column heading.

25. Which one of the following is INCORRECT while selecting multiple cells in MS Excel?
    (A) (A1:G50)
    (B) (A1, B3:C9)
    (C) (A1:B5:C5)
    (D) (A1:B5#C5)

26. In MS-PowerPoint 2007, the picture cropping tool allows you to ________.
    (A) Reset a picture to its default settings
    (B) Change the contrast of a picture
    (C) Recolour a picture
    (D) Remove a portion of a picture

27. In MS-PowerPoint 2007, on the ribbon of which tab would you find Slide Background styles?
    (A) Insert
    (B) Design
    (C) Slide Show
    (D) Home

28. In MS-Word 2007, setting up page margins is done through _______ tab.
    (A) Home
    (B) Page Layout
    (C) View
    (D) Review
29. Which of the following is not a version of the Windows operating system?
    (A) Windows 90
    (B) Windows 98
    (C) Windows Vista
    (D) Windows Me
30. Identify this Semi-Automatic Calculating Device.

    (A) Pascaline
    (B) Staffelwalze
    (C) Jaquard's Loom
    (D) Difference Engine
31. The process of conversion of Digital signals to Analog signals is called _________.
    (A) Modulation
    (B) Demodulation
    (C) Decryption
    (D) Encryption
32. Which feature of MS-Excel 2007, allows you to monitor cells in other worksheets whilst making changes in the current worksheet?
    (A) Data Validation
    (B) Trace Precedents
    (C) Watch Window
    (D) Trace Error

33. Match the following:

Column-I	Column-II
I. Newsgroups	a. Buying and selling products on the internet.
II. E -mail	b. A tool allowing your PC to connect to another network and log in as if you were a user on that system
III. Telnet	c. Discussions on the internet on a range of topics – recreational to research
IV. E-commerce	d. Sending and receiving messages in electronic form over the internet

    (A) I – c, II – a, III – d, IV – b
    (B) I – c, II – d, III – b, IV – a
    (C) I – c, II – a, III – b, IV – d
    (D) I – a, II – c, III – d, IV – b
34. What is the output of the following HTML code?

```
<html>
<body>
FIRST STATEMENT <BR>
SECOND STATEMENT <BR>
THIRD STATEME NT <BR>
</body>
</html>
```

    (A) FIRST STATEMENT
        SECOND STATEMENT
        THIRD STATEMENT
    (B) FIRST STATEMENT SECOND STATEMENT THIRD STATEMENT
    (C) FIRST STATEMENT
        THIRD STATEMENT
        SECOND STATEMENT
    (D) **FIRST STATEMENT
        SECOND STATEMENT
        THIRD STATEMENT**
35. In MS-Excel 2007, which of the following function returns the current date?
    (A) TODAY   (B) DATE
    (C) DATEVALUE   (D) TODAYSDATE

36. In MS-PowerPoint 2007, which of the following statements about deleting slides is NOT correct?
    (A) Slides can be deleted during a slide show.
    (B) A slide can be deleted by selecting the slide in left panel in normal view and clicking the Delete button on the Home tab.
    (C) A slide can be deleted by selecting the slide in Slide Sorter view and pressing .
    (D) A slide must be selected before it can be deleted.

37. In MS-Excel 2007, the procedure to select a range of cells is _________.
    (A) Click on first desired cell + press shift + click on last desired cell
    (B) Click on first desired cell + press ctrl + click on last desired cell
    (C) Click on first desired cell + press tab + click on last desired cell
    (D) All of these

38. Reel, Cartridge, Streamer and DAT are types of which storage device?
    (A) RAM   (B) EPROM
    (C) Magnetic Tape   (D) Floppy Disk

39. Online communities of people who share interests or activities are called _________.
    (A) E-mail
    (B) E-Commerce
    (C) Web Servers
    (D) Social Networks

40. Match the following Indent names with the Indent types: (in MS-Word 2007)

Column-I	Column-II
I. Left	a. Indents just the first line of a paragraph from the left margin.
II. Right	b. Indents all but the first line of text from the left margin.
III. First line	c. Indents text from the right margin.
IV. Hanging	d. Indents text from the left margin.

(A) I – d, II – c, III – a, IV – b
(B) I – a, II – d, III – c, IV – b
(C) I – b, II – d, III – c, IV – a
(D) I – a, II – d, III – b, IV – c

41. Which device should be installed in a multimedia PC such that television signals can be received by it?
    (A) TV tuner card
    (B) PC tuner card
    (C) HDMI cable
    (D) PCI express card

42. Identify this device from the description given below:
    i.   Allows user to create digital drawings by hand-drawing images.
    ii. It usually has a flat surface.
    iii. Commonly used for CAD terminals and engineering workstations.
    iv. A special pen called stylus is used to write on it.
    (A) Joystick
    (B) Digitizer tablet
    (C) Touch Screen
    (D) Optical Mark Reader

43. Find the odd one out:
    (A) AVG
    (B) VLC Player
    (C) Winamp
    (D) Media Jukebox

44. What is the HTML syntax to set the font of the text to ARIAL?
    (A) <FONT COLOR=ARIAL>
    (B) <FONT ="ARIAL">
    (C) <FONT FACE="ARIAL">
    (D) <FONT TYPE="ARIAL">

45. Which tab and function in MS-Word 2007 should be used to create a fully-formatted cover page for your document?
    (A) Review → Cover Page
    (B) Page Layout → Cover Page
    (C) Layout → Cover Page
    (D) Insert → Cover Page

46. Memory management technique in which memory is divided into variable

sized chunks which can be allocated to processes is called ___________.

(A) Paging   (B) Segmentation

(C) GDT   (D) Realmode

47. Which part of the CPU performs the (+,–,*,/) and (>, >=, <=, <=, = and <>) operations?

(A) MU   (B) CU

(C) ALU   (D) SU

48. Which of the following statements is correct for Gmail Contacts Manager.

(A) You can search by phone numbers, if entered.

(B) You can search by a person's first and/or last name.

(C) You can search by domain or user name.

(D) All of these

49. In HTML, the links to sections within the same page are called _________.

(A) Interwiki link

(B) Internal link

(C) External link

(D) Anchors

50. You can search the e-mail with the following attachments.

(A) .docx, .pptx, .xlsx files

(B) .bmp, .jpg, .tif, .png files

(C) .zip, .rar files

(D) All of these

—Darken Your Choice with HB Pencil —

1.	Ⓐ Ⓑ Ⓒ Ⓓ	11.	Ⓐ Ⓑ Ⓒ Ⓓ	21.	Ⓐ Ⓑ Ⓒ Ⓓ	31	Ⓐ Ⓑ Ⓒ Ⓓ	41.	Ⓐ Ⓑ Ⓒ Ⓓ
2.	Ⓐ Ⓑ Ⓒ Ⓓ	12.	Ⓐ Ⓑ Ⓒ Ⓓ	22.	Ⓐ Ⓑ Ⓒ Ⓓ	32.	Ⓐ Ⓑ Ⓒ Ⓓ	42.	Ⓐ Ⓑ Ⓒ Ⓓ
3.	Ⓐ Ⓑ Ⓒ Ⓓ	13.	Ⓐ Ⓑ Ⓒ Ⓓ	23.	Ⓐ Ⓑ Ⓒ Ⓓ	33.	Ⓐ Ⓑ Ⓒ Ⓓ	43.	Ⓐ Ⓑ Ⓒ Ⓓ
4.	Ⓐ Ⓑ Ⓒ Ⓓ	14.	Ⓐ Ⓑ Ⓒ Ⓓ	24.	Ⓐ Ⓑ Ⓒ Ⓓ	34.	Ⓐ Ⓑ Ⓒ Ⓓ	44.	Ⓐ Ⓑ Ⓒ Ⓓ
5.	Ⓐ Ⓑ Ⓒ Ⓓ	15.	Ⓐ Ⓑ Ⓒ Ⓓ	25.	Ⓐ Ⓑ Ⓒ Ⓓ	35.	Ⓐ Ⓑ Ⓒ Ⓓ	45.	Ⓐ Ⓑ Ⓒ Ⓓ
6.	Ⓐ Ⓑ Ⓒ Ⓓ	16.	Ⓐ Ⓑ Ⓒ Ⓓ	26.	Ⓐ Ⓑ Ⓒ Ⓓ	36.	Ⓐ Ⓑ Ⓒ Ⓓ	46.	Ⓐ Ⓑ Ⓒ Ⓓ
7.	Ⓐ Ⓑ Ⓒ Ⓓ	17.	Ⓐ Ⓑ Ⓒ Ⓓ	27.	Ⓐ Ⓑ Ⓒ Ⓓ	37.	Ⓐ Ⓑ Ⓒ Ⓓ	47.	Ⓐ Ⓑ Ⓒ Ⓓ
8.	Ⓐ Ⓑ Ⓒ Ⓓ	18.	Ⓐ Ⓑ Ⓒ Ⓓ	28.	Ⓐ Ⓑ Ⓒ Ⓓ	38.	Ⓐ Ⓑ Ⓒ Ⓓ	48.	Ⓐ Ⓑ Ⓒ Ⓓ
9.	Ⓐ Ⓑ Ⓒ Ⓓ	19.	Ⓐ Ⓑ Ⓒ Ⓓ	29.	Ⓐ Ⓑ Ⓒ Ⓓ	39.	Ⓐ Ⓑ Ⓒ Ⓓ	49.	Ⓐ Ⓑ Ⓒ Ⓓ
10.	Ⓐ Ⓑ Ⓒ Ⓓ	20.	Ⓐ Ⓑ Ⓒ Ⓓ	30.	Ⓐ Ⓑ Ⓒ Ⓓ	40.	Ⓐ Ⓑ Ⓒ Ⓓ	50.	Ⓐ Ⓑ Ⓒ Ⓓ

1. FUNDAMENTALS OF COMPUTER

Answer Key

1. (A)	2. (B)	3. (B)	4. (D)	5. (C)	6. (A)	7. (A)	8. (C)	9. (C)	10. (D)
11. (A)	12. (D)	13. (A)	14. (D)	15. (B)	16. (C)	17. (C)	18. (A)	19. (C)	20. (B)
21. (B)	22. (D)	23. (A)	24. (B)	25. (A)	26. (B)	27. (C)	28. (A)	29. (D)	30. (A)

HOTS (ACHIEVERS SECTION)

31. (D)	32. (B)	33. (A)	34. (D)	35. (A)	36. (A)	37. (C)	38. (A)	39. (B)	40. (D)

2. OPERATING SYSTEMS

Answer Key

1. (D)	2. (D)	3. (B)	4. (A)	5. (B)	6. (D)	7. (A)	8. (C)	9. (D)	10. (C)
11. (D)	12. (C)	13. (C)	14. (D)	15. (A)	16. (C)	17. (D)	18. (A)	19. (D)	20. (D)

1. **(D)**

    An Operating System acts as an intermediary between user/user applications/application programs and hardware. It is a program that manages hardware resources. It provides services to application programs.

3. **Answer: (B)**

    To access services of the Operating System an interface is provided by the System Calls. Generally, these are functions written in C and C++. Open, Close, Read, Write are some of most prominently used system calls.

5. **(B)**

    Kernel is the first program that is loaded in memory when OS is loading as well as it remains in memory till OS is running. Kernel is the core part of the OS which is responsible for managing resources, allowing multiple processes to use the resources and provide services to various processes. Kernel modules can be loaded and unloaded in run-time i.e. in running OS.

6. **(D)**

    All the mentioned errors are handled by OS. The OS is continuously monitoring all of its resources. Also, the OS is constantly detecting and correcting errors.

8. (C)

If a process fails, most operating systems write the error information to a log file. Log file is examined by the debugger, to find out what is the actual cause of that particular problem. Log file is useful for system programmers for correcting errors.

9. (D)

In Operating Systems, each process has its own address space which contains code, data, stack, and heap segments or sections. Each process also has a list of files that is opened by the process as well as all pending alarms, signals, and various signal handlers.

10. (C)

In a time-sharing operating system, when the time slot given to a process is completed, the process goes from the running state to the Ready State. In a time-sharing operating system, unit time is defined for sharing CPU, it is called a time quantum or time slice. If a process takes less than 1 time quantum, then the process itself releases the CPU.

11. (D)

Suppose that a process is in "Blocked" state waiting for some I/O service. When the service is completed, it goes to the ready state. Process never goes directly to the running state from the waiting state. Only processes which are in ready state go to the running state whenever CPU allocated by operating system.

13. (C)

In a time sharing system, each user needs to get a share of the CPU at regular intervals.

14. (D)

Resource allocation states are used to maintain the availability of the already and current available resources.

21. (B)	22. (C)	23. (C)	24. (D)	25. (D)

21. (B)

Explanation: Interrupt latency is the time duration between the generation of interrupt and execution of its service.

3. DATABASE MANAGEMENT SYSTEM

Answer Key

1. (D)	2. (A)	3. (B)	4. (B)	5. (C)	6. (A)	7. (C)	8. (D)	9. (A)	10. (B)
11. (A)	12. (C)	13. (D)	14. (B)	15. (B)	16. (D)	17. (D)	18. (B)	19. (A)	20. (D)

21. (D)	22. (C)	23. (A)	24. (C)	25. (C)

4. HTML AND CSS

Answer Key

1. (B)	2. (D)	3. (A)	4. (B)	5. (A)	6. (C)	7. (A)	8. (A)	9. (C)	10. (A)
11. (C)	12. (B)	13. (B)	14. (D)	15. (C)	16. (B)	17. (A)	18. (B)	19. (A)	20. (A)
21. (C)	22. (A)	23. (B)	24. (D)	25. (A)					

HOTS (ACHIEVERS SECTION)

26. (A)	27. (B)	28. (D)	29. (B)	30. (A)

5. MS WORD

Answer Key

1. (C)	2. (A)	3. (D)	4. (D)	5. (D)	6. (D)	7. (C)	8. (B)	9. (C)	10. (C)
11. (C)	12. (A)	13. (A)	14. (A)	15. (B)	16. (C)	17. (A)	18. (B)	19. (C)	20. (A)
21. (B)	22. (D)	23. (A)	24. (A)	25. (A)	26. (A)	27. (B)	28. (C)	29. (A)	30. (C)

HOTS (ACHIEVERS SECTION)

31. (C)	32. (B)	33. (A)	34. (D)	35. (B)

6. MS POWERPOINT

Answer Key

1. (A)	2. (D)	3. (C)	4. (D)	5. (D)	6. (D)	7. (D)	8. (D)	9. (B)	10. (D)
11. (D)	12. (D)	13. (A)	14. (B)	15. (C)	16. (B)	17. (B)	18. (C)	19. (D)	20. (D)
21. (B)	22. (B)	23. (D)	24. (C)	25. (A)	26. (D)	27. (B)	28. (D)	29. (A)	30. (A)

HOTS (ACHIEVERS SECTION)

31. (B)	32. (D)	33. (A)	34. (C)	35. (A)

7. MS EXCEL

Answer Key

1. (B)	2. (D)	3. (D)	4. (A)	5. (C)	6. (D)	7. (A)	8. (D)	9. (B)	10. (C)
11. (D)	12. (B)	13. (C)	14. (C)	15. (B)	16. (C)	17. (B)	18. (A)	19. (D)	20. (C)
21. (B)	22. (D)	23. (B)	24. (C)	25. (C)	26. (D)	27. (B)	28. (D)	29. (A)	30. (B)

HOTS (ACHIEVERS SECTION)

31. (A)	32. (B)	33. (D)	34. (D)	35. (A)

8. INTERNET AND VIRUSES

Answer Key

1. (C)	2. (A)	3. (C)	4. (B)	5. (C)	6. (B)	7. (B)	8. (B)	9. (D)	10. (C)
11. (C)	12. (B)	13. (A)	14. (A)	15. (D)	16. (D)	17. (D)	18. (A)	19. (D)	20. (B)
21. (B)	22. (D)	23. (C)	24. (A)	25. (C)	26. (C)	27. (B)	28. (D)	29. (B)	30. (C)

HOTS (ACHIEVERS SECTION)

31. (C)	32. (C)	33. (C)	34. (B)	35. (B)

9. NETWORKING AND MULTIMEDIA

Answer Key

1. (D)	2. (D)	3. (C)	4. (A)	5. (A)	6. (D)	7. (B)	8. (B)	9. (A)	10. (A)
11. (A)	12. (C)	13. (A)	14. (B)	15. (C)	16. (A)	17. (B)	18. (A)	19. (D)	20. (C)
21. (A)	22. (C)	23. (A)	24. (B)	25. (C)	26. (B)	27. (C)	28. (A)	29. (D)	30. (A)

HOTS (ACHIEVERS SECTION)

31. (B)	32. (A)	33. (D)	34. (A)	35. (B)

Answer Key

1. (A)	2. (B)	3. (D)	4. (C)	5. (B)	6. (B)	7. (A)	8. (B)	9. (A)	10. (B)
11. (C)	12. (B)	13. (C)	14. (D)	15. (B)					

1. **(A)**

   Scratch is a visual programming language created by the MIT Media Lab in 2007. Its a drag-and-drop interface with colorful blocks makes it one of the most intuitive programming languages to learn.

2. **(B)**

   Sprite: An object in Scratch which performs functions controlled by scripts.

   Squeak: The environment in which Scratch runs and is programmed in.

3. **(D)**

   A backdrop is an image that can be shown on the Stage. It is similar to a costume, except that it is shown on the stage instead. They are located in the backdrops library. The Stage can change its look to any of its backdrops using the Switch Backdrop to () block.

4. **(C)**

   A script is a collection or stack of blocks that all interlock with one another. The blocks and their order are very important, as they determine how sprites interact with each other and the backdrop.

5. **(B)**

   A costume is one out of possibly many "frames" or alternate appearances of a sprite. Sprites can change their look to any of its costumes. They can be named, edited, created, and deleted, but every sprite must have at least one costume.

6. **(B)**

   Tempo is measured in BPM, or beats per minute. One beat every second is 60 BPM. Sometimes the tempo is written at the beginning of the music and is called a metronome marking. Tempo and stylistic feel are often indicated in classical music by Italian terminology.

7. **(A)**

   The Stage can change its look to any of its backdrops using the Switch Backdrop to () block.

8. **(B)**

   A script is defined within the Scratch program as one or a set of blocks that begins with a Hat Block. Even a single block can qualify. However, scripts are usually referred to as sets of blocks that consist of at least two blocks.

9. **(A)**

   Unlike Scratch 1.4 files, Scratch 2.0 files are ZIP archives containing project information encoded in a text-based format called JSON and project media in separate files. Projects conventionally have the extension . sb2 , and sprites the extension . sprite2 .

10. **(B)**

    The Switch Costume to () block is a Looks block and a Stack block that changes its sprite's costume to a specified one. This block is used whenever a sprite must switch to a specific costume (instead of the next costume block, which only switches to the next costume in the costume list).

11. **(C)**

    The When Green Flag Clicked block, commonly called the Start Block, is an Events block and a Hat block. Scripts that wear this block will activate once the Green Flag has been clicked — these scripts can activate other scripts and enable the entire program.

12. (B)

The move () steps block is a stack block and a Motion block. The block moves its sprite forward the specified amount of steps in the direction it is facing. A step is equal to a one-pixel length. The Default Value is 10 and can be replaced by any number.

13. (C)

The Forever If () block is a Control block and a C block. The block would continuously check its Boolean condition. If the condition is true, the code held inside the block would run, and then the script continues, but if the condition is false, nothing would happen until it becomes true again.

14. (D)

Motion blocks is one of the ten categories of Scratch blocks. They are color-coded medium-blue and are used to control a sprite's movement. They are available only for sprites. There are currently 18 Motion blocks: 15 stack blocks and 3 reporter blocks.

15. (B)

Control blocks is one of the nine categories of Scratch blocks. They are color-coded gold, and are used to control scripts. In Scratch 1.4 and earlier, this category also included the blocks that are now Events Blocks.

HOTS (ACHIEVERS SECTION)

16. (B)	17. (B)	18. (D)	19. (C)	20. (D)

11. PROGRAMMING IN PYTHON

Answer Key

1. (C)	2. (D)	3. (B)	4. (C)	5. (A)	6. (D)	7. (A)	8. (A)	9. (B)	10. (B)
11. (D)	12. (C)	13. (D)	14. (A)	15. (C)	16. (B)	17. (B)	18. (B)	19. (B)	20. (A)
21. (D)	22. (C)	23. (D)	24. (B)	25. (C)	26. (C)	27. (A)	28. (B)	29. (C)	30. (B)

1. (C)

Python language is designed by a Dutch programmer Guido van Rossum in the Netherlands.

2. (D)

Python is an interpreted programming language, which supports object-oriented, structured, and functional programming.

3. (B)

Case is always significant while dealing with identifiers in python.

4. (C)

'.py' is the correct extension of the Python file. Python programs can be written in any text editor. To save these programs we need to save in files with file extension '.py'.

5. (A)

Many languages have been implemented using both compilers and interpreters, including C, Pascal, and Python.

6. (D)

True, False and None are capitalized while the others are in lower case.

7. (A)

The order of precedence is: %, +. Hence the expression above, on simplification results in 4 + 3 = 7. Hence the result is 7.

8. (A)

In Python, to define a block of code we use indentation. Indentation refers to whitespaces at the beginning of the line.

9. (B)

The def keyword is used to create, (or define) a function in python.

10. (B)

To write single-line comments in Python use the Hash character (#) at the beginning of the line. It is also called number sign or pound sign. To write multi-line comments, close the text between triple quotes.
Example: """ comment
text """

11. (D)

The function sys.version can help us to find the version of python that we are currently working on. It also contains information on the build number and compiler used. For example, 3.5.2, 2.7.3 etc. this function also returns the current date, time, bits etc along with the version.

12. (C)

Python supports the creation of anonymous functions (i.e. functions that are not bound to a name) at runtime, using a construct called lambda. Lambda functions are restricted to a single expression. They can be used wherever normal functions can be used.

13. (D)

For order of precedence, just remember this PEMDAS (similar to BODMAS).

14. (A)

The binary form of 1 is 0001. The expression x<<2 implies we are performing bitwise left shift on x. This shift yields the value: 0100, which is the binary form of the number 4.

15. (C)

PIP is a package manager for python. Which is also called Preferred Installer Program.

16. (B)

Variable names can be of any length.

17. (B)

// is the operator for truncation division. It is called so because it returns only the integer part of the quotient, truncating the decimal part. For example: 20//3 = 6.

18. (B)

The function seed is a function which is present in the random module. The functions sqrt and factorial are a part of the math module. The print function is a built-in function which prints a value directly to the system output.

19. (B)

Each object in Python has a unique id. The id() function returns the object's id.

20. (A)

The code shown above shows a general decorator which can work with any number of arguments.

21. (D)

The function max() is being used to find the maximum value from among –3, –4 and false. Since false amounts to the value zero, hence we are left with min(0, 2, 7). Hence the output is 0 (false).

22. (C)

Class is a user-defined data type.

23. (D)

The expression shown above rounds off the given number to the number of decimal places specified. Since the expression given specifies rounding off to two decimal places, the output of this expression will be 56.24. Had the value been x = 56.234 (last digit being any number less than 5), the output would have been 56.23.

24. (B)

A folder of python programs is called as a package of modules.

25. (C)

The function len() returns the length of the number of elements in the iterable. Therefore the output of the function shown above is 4.

26. (C)

Python first searches for the local, then the global and finally the built-in namespace.

27. (A)

[::-1] reverses the list.

28. (B)

+ operator is concatenation operator.

29. (C)

Both str(f) and format(f) call f.__str__().

30. (B)

eval can be used as a variable.

HOTS (ACHIEVERS SECTION)

| 31. (C) | 32. (B) | 33. (C) | 34. (C) | 35. (B) |

31. (C)

The else part is not executed if control breaks out of the loop

32. (B)

The output that is required is 6, that is, row 2, item 3. This position is represented by the statement: A[1][2].

33. (C)

Lists should be copied by executing [:] operation

34. (C)

The code shown above returns a new list containing only those elements of the list l which do not amount to zero. Hence the output is: [1, 2, 'hello'].

35. (B)

SyntaxError, there shouldn't be a space between + and = in +=

12. LATEST DEVELOPMENTS IN THE FIELD OF 'IT'

Answer Key

| 1. (B) | 2. (A) | 3. (D) | 4. (D) | 5. (C) | 6. (B) | 7. (B) | 8. (A) | 9. (A) | 10. (C) |
| 11. (C) | 12. (B) | 13. (C) | 14. (D) | 15. (C) | 16. (B) | 17. (D) | 18. (B) | 19. (A) | 20. (D) |

1. **(B)**

The Daydream View headset is made with lightweight fabric, designed and built for virtual reality.

9. **(A)**

IPS (Indoor Positioning System) can be used to locate people or objects inside buildings, typically via a mobile device such as a smart phone or tablet.

12. **(B)**

Kinect is a line of Motion Sensing input device, developed by Microsoft. Motion sensing is the process of detecting a change in the position of an object relative to its surroundings.

14. **(D)**

Google keep is a note-taking service, developed by Google

16. **(B)**

Chrome cast is a line of digital media players developed by Google.

HOTS (ACHIEVERS SECTION)

21. (B)	22. (C)	23. (D)	24. (A)	25. (B)

13. LOGICAL REASONING

Answer Key

1. (A)	2. (D)	3. (B)	4. (D)	5. (D)	6. (C)	7. (D)	8. (C)	9. (D)	10. (C)
11. (C)	12. (D)	13. (D)	14. (A)	15. (C)	16. (A)	17. (A)	18. (D)	19. (C)	20. (C)
21. (C)	22. (B)	23. (B)	24. (D)	25. (D)	26. (C)	27. (B)	28. (B)	29. (B)	30. (B)
31. (A)	32. (B)	33. (C)	34. (D)	35. (A)	36. (D)	37. (C)	38. (B)	39. (D)	40. (D)
41. (C)	42. (D)	43. (D)	44. (C)	45. (C)	46. (D)	47. (C)	48. (C)	49. (C)	50. (A)
51. (D)	52. (C)	53. (C)	54. (D)	55. (A)	56. (C)	57. (D)	58. (B)	59. (C)	60. (A)

1. **(A)**

A 'bank' deals with transaction of 'money'. Likewise, 'transport' deals with the movement of 'goods'.

3. **(B)**

Needle is related to clock as wheel is related to vehicle.

5. **(D)**

As, boat is sailed by oar in the same way, a bicycle is driven by pedal.

7. **(D)**

Yen, Lira and Dollar are currency. Ounce is used for weight.

8. **(C)**

Huge, tiny and small are size whereas heavy is used to measure weight.

9. **(D)**

Teeth, tongue and palate are inside the mouth. chin is outside.

11. **(C)**

$a[0] = 6 + 0 + (-4) = 2$

$a[1] = 6 + 6 + (-4 + 0) = 8$

$a[2] = 6 + 12 + (-4 + 0 + 4) = 18$

$a[3] = 6 + 18 + (-4 + 0 + 4 + 8) = 32$

$a[4] = 6 + 24 + (-4 + 0 + 4 + 8 + 12) = 50$

13. (D)

$14 = 2^2$

$316 = 4^2$

$536 = 6^2$

$764 = 8^2$

$9100 = 10^2$

$11144 = 12^2$

15. (C)

So, the sequence is defined by a(n) = a(n1)*a (n − 2), where a (0) = 2 and a(1) = 3, so a(5) = a (4)*a(3) where a(3) = 18 and a(5) = 1944, therefore a(4) = 108.

17. (A)

As

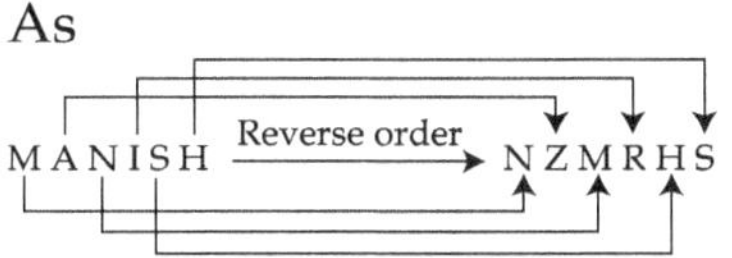

In the same way,

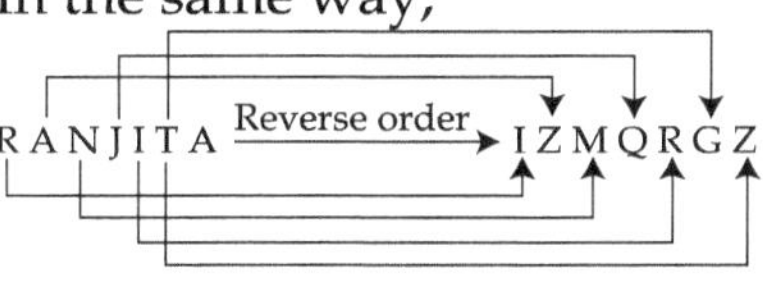

18. (D)

Each letter is represented by its preceding and following letter.

20. (C)

Last two letters of the word CDPQYZ are the next two letters of the last letter of the word BOX.

21. (C)

Alphabetical order is Place < Plain < Plane < Player.

24. (D)

E X P E R I E N C E D

26. (C)

The daughter of Akash's father's wife is the sister of Akash and brother of the daughter is the brother of Akash.

27. (B)

Only daughter of Neha's father is Neha herself. In other words, neha is the mother of that man.

28. (B)

M is the maternal uncle of R means M is the brother of the mother (say K) of R i.e. M + K − R.

33. (C)

Let X and Y be two buses. Bus X travels the PA, AB, BC, CD.

Now, AD = BC = 25 km.

So, PD = PA + AD = 50 km.

Bus Y travels 35 km upto E.

Distance between two buses

= PQ − (PD + QE) = [150 − (50 + 35)]

= 65 km.

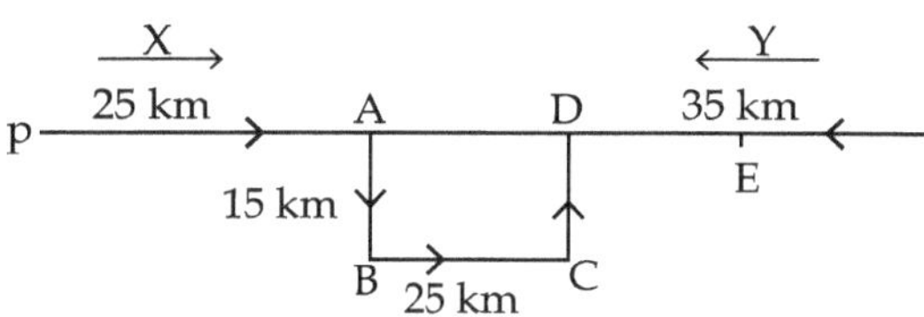

37. (C)

Two months will have the same calender if the period between them is divisible by 7.

Now,

(A) June + July + Aug. + Sep.

= 30 + 31 + 31 + 30

= 122 (not divisible by 7)

(B) Apr. + May + June + July + Aug. + Sep. + Oct.

= 30 + 31 + 30 + 31 + 31 +30 + 31

= 213 (not divisible by 7)

(C) Apr. + May + June

= 30 + 31 + 30 = 91 (divisible by 7)

(D) October + November

= 31 + 30 = 61 (not divisible by 7)

38. (D)

In 1962, on 17th November it is Saturday. So, in 1963, 17th November will be Sunday and in 1964, 17th November should be Monday but as it is leap year so it will be Tuesday. On 22nd November, 1963 therefore, will be Sunday.

41. (C)

The symbols move in the sequence ⟨K⟩ in the first step. In each subsequent step, the symbols move in the sequence obtained by rotating the previous sequence through 90° ACW. Also, in each step, the symbol that reaches the encircled position gets replaced by a new one.

42. (D)

In each step, the first element moves to the third position and gets replaced by a new element; the second and the third elements move to the first and the second positions respectively and the entire figure rotates by 90°.

43. (D)

In each step, all the elements move to the adjacent corner (of the square boundary) in a CW direction and the element that reaches the upper-left corner gets vertically inverted.

44. (C)

We can label the arcs as shown ⟨¹₂₃₄₅₆⟩. The arcs get inverted in the sequence (1 & 2), (3, 4 & 5), (6 & 1), (2, 3 & 4), (5 & 6).

45. (C)

In each step, one line segment is lost from the CW-end of the outer element and a new line segment appears at the ACW-end. Also, the inner 'L' shaped element rotates 90° in each step.

51. (D)

If the cube is cut into 125 smaller cubes, how are the cuts made? 4 cuts/slices in x, y, z-planes respectively. So the cube is a 5 × 5 × 5 cube. That is, it has 5 squares on each of its faces.

So if only one face is painted pink, how many cubes have at least 1 face colored in pink? It is the number of cubes with only one side colored in pink because pink is only colored on one face. So, the answer would be: $5 \times 5 = 25$

52. (C)

Now we know that 2 adjacent faces are not painted. We know for sure that all the cubes which are present in the center of the bigger cube, i.e., all the cubes that are not visible to human eye are not colored. Number of such cubes are: $3 * 3 * 3 = 27$. But there are also some cubes which are visible to us on the sides which are left uncolored. Number of such cubes are: $4 * 3 + 3 * 3 = 21$. Do not count the cubes on the uncolored edges twice while doing this calculation. So total uncolored cubes: $27 + 21 = 48$

You can solve this in a simpler manner if you imagine that, uncolored cubes will be in the form of a $4 \times 4 \times 3$ cube, which gives us 48 uncolored cubes.

53. (C)

There will be at least two faces coloured on 21 cubes.

54. (D)

Only one face colored.

55. (A)

Only one face colored.

Answer Key

1. (C)	2. (B)	3. (D)	4. (A)	5. (D)	6. (A)	7. (B)	8. (D)	9. (B)	10. (A)
11. (D)	12. (C)	13. (D)	14. (D)	15. (A)	16. (B)	17. (C)	18. (C)	19. (A)	20. (C)
21. (A)	22. (D)	23. (B)	24. (A)	25. (D)	26. (D)	27. (B)	28. (B)	29. (A)	30. (C)
31. (A)	32. (C)	33. (B)	34. (A)	35. (A)	36. (A)	37. (A)	38. (C)	39. (D)	40. (A)
41. (A)	42. (B)	43. (A)	44. (C)	45. (D)	46. (B)	47. (C)	48. (D)	49. (D)	50. (D)

SAMPLE OMR ANSWER SHEET

1. STUDENT NAME (IN ENGLISH CAPITAL LETTERS ONLY)

Students must write and darken the respective circles completely using HB Pencil only. Othewise their Answer Sheets will not be evaluated.

PERSONAL DETAILS

2. SCHOOL CODE

3. CLASS

4. SECTION

5. ROLL NO.

6. QUESTION PAPER SET

A ◯
B ◯
C ◯
D ◯

7. MOBILE NUMBER

8. GENDER

MALE ◯
FEMALE ◯

9. STREAM
(Only for Class XI and XII Students)

MATHEMATICS ◯
BIOLOGY ◯
OTHERS ◯

MARK YOUR ANSWERS

No.	A	B	C	D	No.	A	B	C	D
1.	Ⓐ	Ⓑ	Ⓒ	Ⓓ	26.	Ⓐ	Ⓑ	Ⓒ	Ⓓ
2.	Ⓐ	Ⓑ	Ⓒ	Ⓓ	27.	Ⓐ	Ⓑ	Ⓒ	Ⓓ
3.	Ⓐ	Ⓑ	Ⓒ	Ⓓ	28.	Ⓐ	Ⓑ	Ⓒ	Ⓓ
4.	Ⓐ	Ⓑ	Ⓒ	Ⓓ	29.	Ⓐ	Ⓑ	Ⓒ	Ⓓ
5.	Ⓐ	Ⓑ	Ⓒ	Ⓓ	30.	Ⓐ	Ⓑ	Ⓒ	Ⓓ
6.	Ⓐ	Ⓑ	Ⓒ	Ⓓ	31.	Ⓐ	Ⓑ	Ⓒ	Ⓓ
7.	Ⓐ	Ⓑ	Ⓒ	Ⓓ	32.	Ⓐ	Ⓑ	Ⓒ	Ⓓ
8.	Ⓐ	Ⓑ	Ⓒ	Ⓓ	33.	Ⓐ	Ⓑ	Ⓒ	Ⓓ
9.	Ⓐ	Ⓑ	Ⓒ	Ⓓ	34.	Ⓐ	Ⓑ	Ⓒ	Ⓓ
10.	Ⓐ	Ⓑ	Ⓒ	Ⓓ	35.	Ⓐ	Ⓑ	Ⓒ	Ⓓ
11.	Ⓐ	Ⓑ	Ⓒ	Ⓓ	36.	Ⓐ	Ⓑ	Ⓒ	Ⓓ
12.	Ⓐ	Ⓑ	Ⓒ	Ⓓ	37.	Ⓐ	Ⓑ	Ⓒ	Ⓓ
13.	Ⓐ	Ⓑ	Ⓒ	Ⓓ	38.	Ⓐ	Ⓑ	Ⓒ	Ⓓ
14.	Ⓐ	Ⓑ	Ⓒ	Ⓓ	39.	Ⓐ	Ⓑ	Ⓒ	Ⓓ
15.	Ⓐ	Ⓑ	Ⓒ	Ⓓ	40.	Ⓐ	Ⓑ	Ⓒ	Ⓓ
16.	Ⓐ	Ⓑ	Ⓒ	Ⓓ	41.	Ⓐ	Ⓑ	Ⓒ	Ⓓ
17.	Ⓐ	Ⓑ	Ⓒ	Ⓓ	42.	Ⓐ	Ⓑ	Ⓒ	Ⓓ
18.	Ⓐ	Ⓑ	Ⓒ	Ⓓ	43.	Ⓐ	Ⓑ	Ⓒ	Ⓓ
19.	Ⓐ	Ⓑ	Ⓒ	Ⓓ	44.	Ⓐ	Ⓑ	Ⓒ	Ⓓ
20.	Ⓐ	Ⓑ	Ⓒ	Ⓓ	45.	Ⓐ	Ⓑ	Ⓒ	Ⓓ
21.	Ⓐ	Ⓑ	Ⓒ	Ⓓ	46.	Ⓐ	Ⓑ	Ⓒ	Ⓓ
22.	Ⓐ	Ⓑ	Ⓒ	Ⓓ	47.	Ⓐ	Ⓑ	Ⓒ	Ⓓ
23.	Ⓐ	Ⓑ	Ⓒ	Ⓓ	48.	Ⓐ	Ⓑ	Ⓒ	Ⓓ
24.	Ⓐ	Ⓑ	Ⓒ	Ⓓ	49.	Ⓐ	Ⓑ	Ⓒ	Ⓓ
25.	Ⓐ	Ⓑ	Ⓒ	Ⓓ	50.	Ⓐ	Ⓑ	Ⓒ	Ⓓ

Signature of the Student & Date of Examination

Signature of the Invigilator & Date of Examination

V&S Publishers, F-2/16 Ansari Road, Daryaganj, New Delhi-110002, ☎ 011-23240026-27
✉ info@vspublishers.com, 🌐 www.vspublishers.com